An Illustrated History of TAYSIDE'S RAILWAYS DUNDEE and PERTH

By
W A C Smith
Paul Anderson

With the completion of a new stretch of railway there was usually some sort of ceremony. Across Britain, this happened every other week in mid-Victorian times. Local dignitaries, officials, navvies and onlookers posed for the camera as Dollar station was formally opened on 1st May 1869, two days before regular services began. Photograph National Railway Museum.

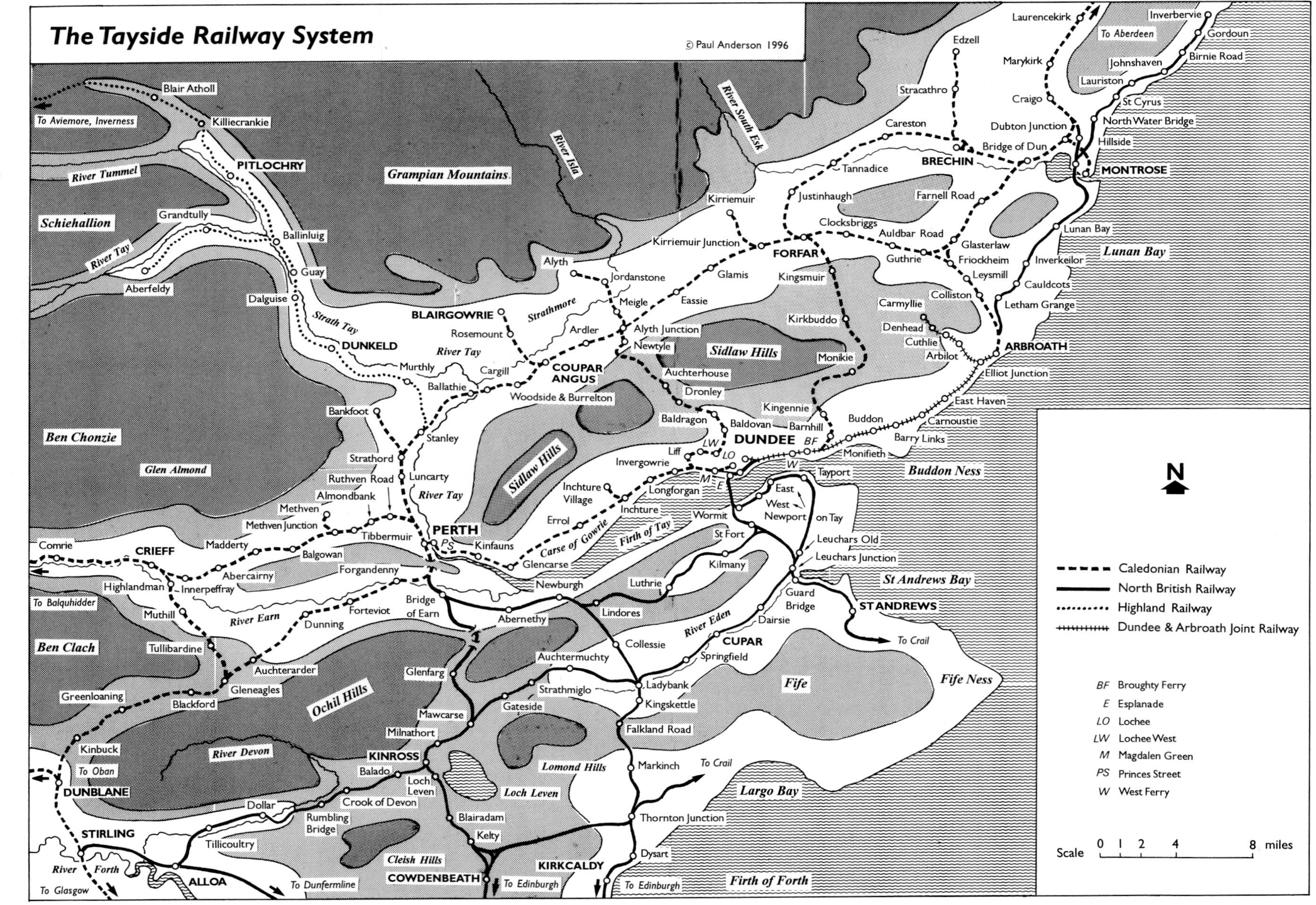
The Tayside Railway System
© Paul Anderson 1996
Caledonian Railway
North British Railway
Highland Railway
Dundee & Arbroath Joint Railway
BF Broughty Ferry
E Esplanade
LO Lochee
LW Lochee West
M Magdalen Green
PS Princes Street
W West Ferry
N
Scale 0 1 2 4 8 miles
To Aviemore, Inverness
Blair Atholl
Killiecrankie
PITLOCHRY
River Tummel
Schiehallion
Grandtully
River Tay
Ballinluig
Aberfeldy
Guay
Dalguise
Strath Tay
DUNKELD
Murthly
Grampian Mountains
River Isla
River South Esk
Alyth
Jordanstone
Meigle
BLAIRGOWRIE
Rosemount
Strathmore
Ardler
Alyth Junction
Newtyle
River Tay
Cargill
COUPAR ANGUS
Ballathie
Woodside & Burrelton
Bankfoot
Stanley
Ben Chonzie
Glen Almond
Strathord
Ruthven Road
Luncarty
Almondbank
Methven
Methven Junction
Tibbermuir
PERTH
PS
Kinfauns
Comrie
CRIEFF
Madderty
Balgowan
Abercairny
Forgandenny
Highlandman
Innerpeffray
To Balquhidder
Muthill
River Earn
Forteviot
Dunning
Bridge of Earn
Ben Clach
Tullibardine
Auchterarder
Gleneagles
Greenloaning
Blackford
Ochil Hills
Kinbuck
To Oban
DUNBLANE
River Devon
STIRLING
River Forth
To Glasgow
ALLOA
Tillicoultry
Dollar
Rumbling Bridge
Crook of Devon
To Dunfermline
Balado
KINROSS
Milnathort
Mawcarse
Glenfarg
Loch Leven
Blairadam
Kelty
Cleish Hills
COWDENBEATH
To Edinburgh
KIRKCALDY
To Edinburgh
Firth of Forth
Dysart
Thornton Junction
Markinch
To Crail
Largo Bay
Loch Leven
Lomond Hills
Falkland Road
Kingskettle
Ladybank
Gateside
Strathmiglo
Auchtermuchty
Abernethy
Newburgh
Lindores
Collessie
Springfield
CUPAR
River Eden
Dairsie
Guard Bridge
Fife
Fife Ness
To Crail
ST ANDREWS
St Andrews Bay
Leuchars Junction
Leuchars Old
Kilmany
Luthrie
St Fort
Wormit
Newport on Tay
West
East
Tayport
Firth of Tay
Carse of Gowrie
Glencarse
Errol
Inchture
Inchture Village
Longforgan
Invergowrie
Liff
LW
LO
M
E
W
DUNDEE
BF
Baldovan
Barnhill
Baldragon
Kingennie
Dronley
Auchterhouse
Sidlaw Hills
Sidlaw Hills
Monifieth
Buddon Ness
Barry Links
Buddon
Carnoustie
East Haven
Elliot Junction
ARBROATH
Arbirlot
Cuthlie
Denhead
Carmyllie
Colliston
Monikie
Kirkbuddo
Kingsmuir
FORFAR
Glamis
Eassie
Kirriemuir Junction
Kirriemuir
Justinhaugh
Clocksbriggs
Auldbar Road
Guthrie
Glasterlaw
Friockheim
Leysmill
Letham Grange
Cauldcots
Inverkeilor
Lunan Bay
Lunan Bay
Farnell Road
Tannadice
BRECHIN
Careston
Stracathro
Edzell
Bridge of Dun
Dubton Junction
Craigo
Marykirk
Laurencekirk
MONTROSE
Hillside
North Water Bridge
St Cyrus
Lauriston
Johnshaven
To Aberdeen
Birnie Road
Gordoun
Inverbervie

ISBN 1-871608-73-2

CONTENTS

Acknowledgements

The authors would like to thank F W Shuttleworth for processing the photographs. All are the copyright of W A C Smith unless credited otherwise. Paul Anderson would like to thank Allison Bennett for typesetting the maps and photocopying, and Juliet Whitworth for undertaking the drawings. W A C Smith wishes to pay especial thanks to Doris for her help, encouragement and patience during the preparation of this book.

First Published in the United Kingdom by
IRWELL PRESS 1997
59A, High Street, Clophill, Bedfordshire MK45 4BE
Printed in Huddersfield by The Amadeus Press

Tayside had several delightful branch lines. In spring sunshine on 23rd May 1955, ex-Caledonian 0-4-4T No 55212 runs round after arrival at Aberfeldy, prior to shunting three coal wagons and a brake van into the yard. Together with the single passenger coach they had formed the 1.02pm mixed train from Ballinluig.

INTRODUCTION
TAYSIDE AND ITS RAILWAYS

Perth General was at its most colourful in Edwardian years, with Highland, Caledonian and North British expresses showing off their various liveries. Highland 4-6-0 No 145 MURTHLY CASTLE in sparkling condition heads past the Glasgow Road ticket platform at Perth with an Inverness train in the early 1900s. Photograph courtesy J F Ward.

Ben Lui towers above the West Highland and Oban lines as they make their way north through Tyndrum. Its bare 3,708ft summit of ancient frost-shattered rocks is covered by snow for nine months of the year and often has a blanket of rain clouds during the summer. Trickles of water emerge from beneath the boulders and combine to form the Fillan Burn which rushes down the lower slopes towards Crianlarich. Scores of tributaries swell the flow and it eventually becomes the River Dochart. At Killin the River Lochay comes in, then a great glacial trough traps the water, creating beautiful Loch Tay below the massive bulk of 3,984ft Ben Lawers. The river escapes at Kenmore, by now bearing the name Tay.

Progress towards the lowlands continues past Aberfeldy and through a deep wooded valley to Ballinluig. Here, the Tay is joined by the River Tummel which brings water from as far away as Rannoch Moor and the Forest of Atholl just a few miles from the roof of Scotland at Cairn Gorm. At Dunkeld the Grampian mountains recede and the river broadens out to meander across a fertile plain. The River Isla comes in west of Coupar Angus, having drained Strathmore, the Forest of Alyth and the Sidlaw Hills, whilst the River Almond joins just before Perth. By now the River Tay is tidal and begins to form an estuary. A final contribution is made by the River Earn which has collected water from the Ochil Hills and the mountains west of Crieff.

With the Carse of Gowrie to the north and Fife to the south, the Tay estuary first widens to three miles then narrows again between Dundee and Newport-on-Tay. The trickle that began over a hundred miles away on the slopes of Ben Lui has become a huge body of water merging with the North Sea. On the Angus shore, the coast stretches away to Carnoustie, Arbroath and Montrose. To the south lie the Eden estuary, St Andrews and Fife Ness.

This book is about the railway system which served Perthshire, Angus, Kinross-shire and northern Fife, a beautiful and immensely varied part of Scotland which has Strath Tay and the Tay Estuary as a common theme. It is a sizeable area: the distance from Dunblane in the south west to Montrose in the north east is 65 miles, and Blair Atholl in the Highlands is 50 miles from Cowdenbeath in the Fife coalfield. It is possible, therefore, only to take a brief look at individual lines.

Diverse geology is the basis for the changing landscape. North of the Highland Boundary Fault from Crieff to Stonehaven, the mountains consist of schist and gneiss - tough rocks which are among the oldest in the British Isles. Old Red Sandstone gives rise to the lush lowlands of Strathmore and Strath Eden, whilst Carboniferous strata from St Andrews to Alloa include a large pocket of coal seams south of Kinross. Massive piles of basalt lavas form the Sidlaw Hills and Ochil Hills, and deep seated cores of ancient volcanoes have been revealed at Dundee Law and the Lomond Hills. In recent geological times, glaciers and rivers have shaped the surface to create the glens and valleys which so often determined the course of Tayside's railways.

Few areas of comparable size can boast such variations in scenery - from the heather covered slopes of the Grampians to the fruit fields of Carse of Gowrie, or from the wooded gorge at Rumbling Bridge to the sandy links at Carnoustie. Towns and villages are equally diverse. On the coast, Arbroath is a long established fishing community famous for its kippers, whilst St Andrews has the oldest academic institution in Scotland. Inland, Crieff had a touch of the wild west about it when cattle droves from the Highlands passed through, whilst Blairgowrie was an early centre for water-powered factories.

Two cities have long dominated Tayside, and they were the pivots of the railway network. Perth began as an insignificant Roman fort called Bertha at the confluence of the Almond and Tay, but by 1100 there was a flourishing settlement on the present site - at the head of navigation. Three centuries later the harbour was very busy and St John's kirk dominated a cramped yet vibrant medieval town. Perth became increasingly important as the focus of natural routeways and prospered accordingly, fine Georgian buildings dating from the late 1700s and early 1800s reflecting the affluence. The town was bound to attract railways but initially promoters had to overcome strong opposition, from local interests wishing to protect both the harbour and the more dignified districts.

Hemmed in by the Sidlaw Hills and Tay estuary, Dundee had none of the natural advantages of Perth, except that its harbour was nearer the sea. However, there was an Iron Age fort on the Law before Bertha camp was established. By the 1100s Dundee was a fishing village which also exported skins and grain to Flanders, the boats bringing back flax and wine. From the mid-1500s there was a golden age when wool and linen manufacturing flourished, but this ended when the town was totally destroyed during the Civil War. The revival of the linen industry had brought renewed prosperity by the late 1700s and a few decades later Dundee embraced railways with enthusiasm.

The town had one of the earliest lines in Scotland and built locomotives almost from the outset. General engineering soon followed and shipbuilding developed during the 1880s. By this time Dundee was one of the world's major whaling ports. Meanwhile, huge mills manufacturing rope, sacking and coarse cloth from Indian jute were being built throughout the city and workers lured from the Highlands and Ireland found accommodation in tenements every bit as dour as those in Glasgow.

Tayside's comprehensive railway network emerged in six identifiable phases spanning the eight decades from 1830 to 1910. They broadly followed the pattern elsewhere in Britain, though of course there were local variations. The six categories can be summarised as follows: Pioneers (1830-39); Trunk Routes (1840-50); Branches (1851-65); Links (1866-1881); Grand Works (1882-90); Marginal Territory (1891-1910). Generally speaking, the lines built during the second phase have proved the most durable.

One of the many branches retained for goods traffic long after passenger services ended was that to Bervie. J37 0-6-0 No 64602 heads past North Water Bridge with the daily trip to the terminus on 18th May 1966. In 1965 the departure time was changed from 13.45 to 10.40 so that the same engine could work the 13.25 trip to Brechin.

Although some remarkable long distance waggonway schemes were mooted around 1820, the first railway actually built was the bold but cumbersome Dundee & Newtyle of 1831. It was a true pioneer, attempting to satisfy local needs and actually gaining two feeder branches in 1837. The Dundee & Arbroath and Arbroath & Forfar followed in 1838-39. They were more like the conventional railways of later years, but had a non-standard gauge and a parochial outlook reflected by their separate termini in Arbroath.

Several trunk routes were proposed during the early 1840s, but a frantic bout of promotion in the middle of that decade - the infamous Railway Mania - gave rise to the basic Tayside network. After a tremendous amount of construction work, the like of which Scotland had never seen before, the new routes opened almost simultaneously. The Dundee & Perth came first in 1847, followed by the Scottish Central (Stirling to Perth), Scottish Midland Junction (Perth to Forfar) and Edinburgh & Northern (Burntisland to Perth) in 1848. The same year saw the opening of branches to Brechin and Montrose, together with the first part of the Aberdeen Railway, completed in 1850. A line from Ladybank to Tayport, where ferries provided connections to Dundee, was also finished in 1848.

Envious of those places already reaping the advantages of rail transport, virtually every town away from existing routes wanted to join the network. The result was a succession of locally promoted single track branches. St Andrews acquired its railway in 1852, followed by Blairgowrie (1855), Dunkeld (1856), Crieff (1856), Methven (1858), Kinross (1858), Alyth (1861), Kirriemuir (1861), Inverbervie (1865) and Aberfeldy (1865). One line which materialised during this phase was a project delayed from the visionary 1840s - the Highland Railway from Perth to Inverness, completed in 1863.

The mid-1860s saw most of the early companies absorbed by the North British Railway or Caledonian Railway, and these two large concerns were to dominate transport in Tayside for the next sixty years. Promotion and construction had slowed down, new routes tending to be strategic links filling gaps in the network: Methven-Crieff (1866); Dundee-Forfar (1870); Devon Valley (1871); Tayport-Wormit (1879); Arbroath-Kinnaber Junction (1881). The most spectacular link was the Tay Bridge between Wormit and Dundee, opened in 1878. It was also the shortest lived, for the central section collapsed with tragic results at the end of 1879.

With the North British and Caledonian carrying vast amounts of traffic and in ruthless competition with each other, the next decade saw several grand works. Perth station was rebuilt on a massive scale in the early 1880s, the second and much stronger Tay Bridge opened in 1887 and the Forth Bridge, together with a new line through Glenfarg, began to carry trains in 1890. These improvements were followed by the 'Races' to Aberdeen, which in turn prompted a generation of sumptuous passenger coaches and fine locomotives.

The final phase had something in common with the branch line period of 1851-65. This time several villages - even hamlets - away from established tracks gained a railway, but it really was a case of venturing into marginal territory in most instances. Crieff-Comrie opened in 1893 followed by Forfar-Brechin during 1895. A branch reached the village of Edzell in 1896 and isolated countryside around Carmyllie gained a passenger service in 1900. Comrie-Balquhidder (1901-05), the Bankfoot branch (1906) and Newburgh-St Fort (1909) brought the great era of railway construction on Tayside to a close.

In 1923 the North British became part of the London & North Eastern Railway (LNER) and the Caledonian and Highland were absorbed by the London Midland & Scottish Railway (LMS). These, in turn, became part of British Railways in 1948. The subsequent fate of Tayside's railways is outlined in the following chapters. Inevitably, much of the network has been abandoned in the face of competition from road transport. Goods traffic, which sustained many rural lines long after passenger services ceased, is now almost non-existent. However, it is hoped that some of the atmosphere and character of the system in happier days will be conveyed by the wide ranging illustrations. Motorways and trunk roads have cut travelling times significantly, but at least trains were very much in harmony with the braes, straths and carselands of Tayside.

***Top.* Perth became prosperous largely as a result of its harbour, seen here on 20th August 1966. The quays remain busy, although the rail connection (detectable in the foreground) has now been severed.**

***Middle.* A combination of mills and tenements characterised much of inner Dundee. Such was the scene in Lochee Road as tram No 25 headed for Lochee terminus on 20th October 1956, the last day of services.**

***Bottom.* During the 1950s, Tayside's railways were still arteries of commerce. V2 2-6-2 No 60972 climbs away from Montrose with an up freight on 4th July 1959.**

Dundee Ward terminus, probably around the time of its closure in 1861. Note the legend DUNDEE & NEWTYLE RAILWAY STATION above the pleasant stone arcade forming the end wall. The Law appears as a hazy outline in the background and its eastern shoulder was responsible for the incline which began just beyond the twin sheds. Rails across Ward Road in the foreground marked the beginning of the harbour branch. Photograph National Railway Museum.

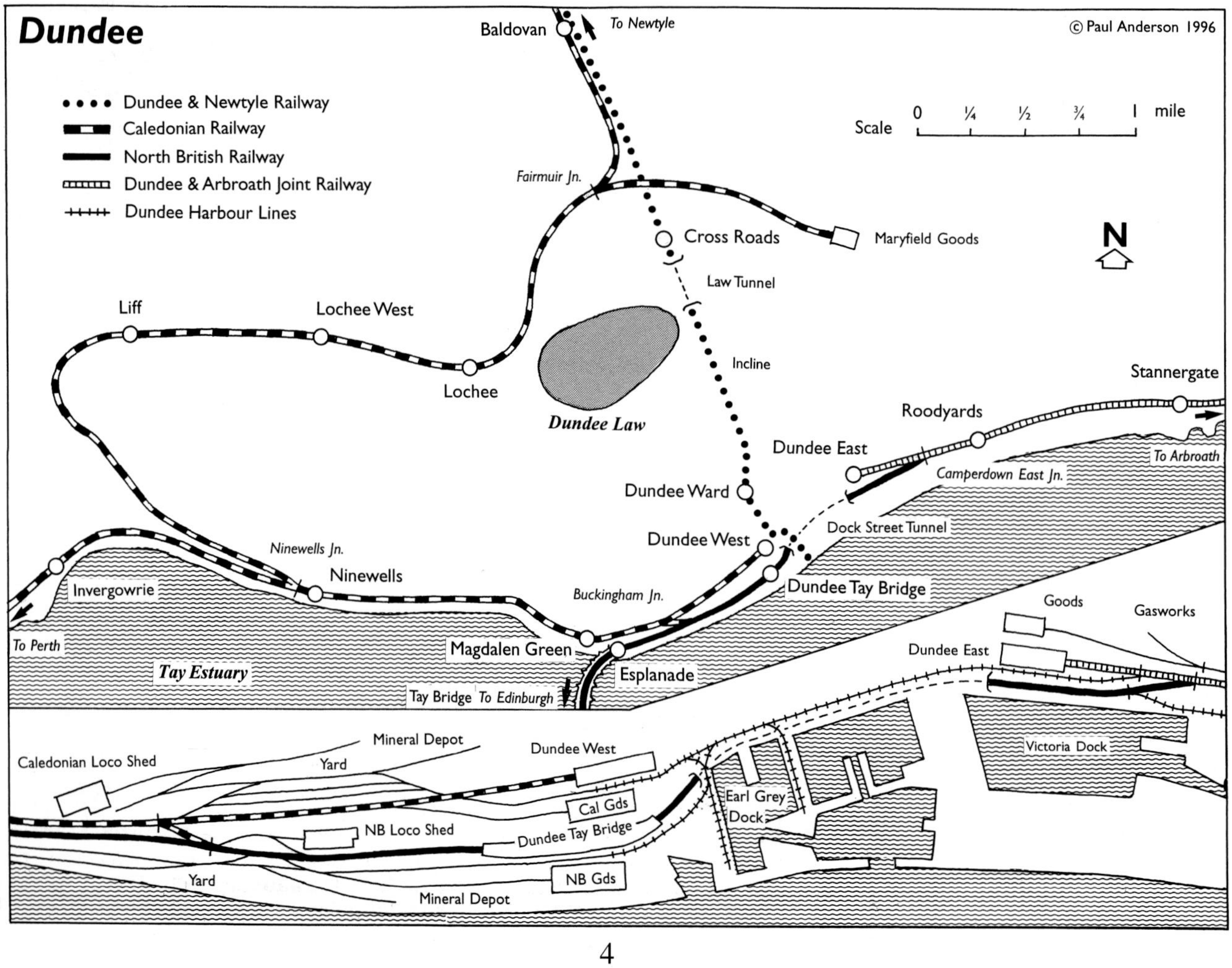

Chapter 1

DUNDEE

There was a neat balance about Dundee's railway system and at times this almost amounted to symmetry, both geographical and historical. Firstly, there were clear cut, unduplicated approaches from the north, south, east and west. These comprised one of Scotland's pioneering routes, an early steam line, a Railway Mania scheme, and one of the boldest pieces of engineering ever attempted. At one time or another the principal stations consisted of a primitive 'depot' with two open sheds, a modest terminus with market town charm, a grand baronial castle of a place, and a claustrophobic island platform below sea level. Anglo-Scottish expresses mixed with residential services, and dock shunters looked on as local trains arrived from remote rural halts. The Dundee & Newtyle was the pioneer and its three rope-worked inclines caused all manner of headaches until they were bypassed. Next came the Dundee & Arbroath which was in a world of its own and even featured right hand running. The Dundee & Perth was conventional enough, but it sprouted one of the strangest branches in Scotland. Finally, the Tay Bridge put Dundee on the main line network, but its catastrophic collapse after just two years was one of the most famous railway disasters of all time. A dock system east of the city centre was balanced by yards and loco sheds to the west, whilst even the new line for Tay Bridge station neatly paralleled an earlier east-west connection through the streets.

DUNDEE & NEWTYLE

Dundee's first railway was once regarded as a quaint little line of purely local interest, but historians eventually agreed that it was an important, if misguided, early enterprise with a much broader significance. During the early 1800s the growing industrial seaport looked north to the Sidlaw Hills for building materials and beyond to fertile Strathmore for agricultural produce. The roads were poor and a canal was suggested in 1817, although this would have been virtually impossible to build. So, in January 1825 the Town Council formed a committee to consider a railway and Charles Landale, described (maybe uniquely!) as an apothecary as well as a civil engineer, was asked to devise a plan. He envisaged an eleven mile line from the northern edge of Dundee to a farmstead called Mill of Newtyle in Strathmore, consisting of three steep inclines with intervening level sections. Besides satisfying Dundee's needs the railway was expected to supply the hinterland with coal, manufactured goods and other requirements. His report was presented in September 1825, before the Stockton & Darlington opened and proved a success. An Act was obtained on 26th May 1826 (at the same time as the Garnkirk & Glasgow and Edinburgh & Dalkeith) and construction work began in February 1827 with local funding. Landowners were enthusiastic and two of them, the Earl of Airlie and Lord Wharncliffe, took over the project from the Town Council.

Landale's scheme depended on very sharp curves round the contours to minimise construction costs, but generous compensation to farmers, extra bridges, and a tunnel under a shoulder of Dundee Law piled on the costs. The partially built Dundee & Newtyle was in deep financial trouble by 1828 and looked at ways of reducing expenditure. Powers to raise more cash came with an Act of 29th May 1830

From 1861 passenger trains over the Dundee & Newtyle began at West station. Tay Bridge B1 4-6-0 No 61101 sent a cloud of steam up to the grimy overall roof as it waited with the 1.12pm from Dundee West to Blairgowrie on 8th January 1955, the last day of service. The young lad seems to be clutching a comic (how appropriate for Dundee!) but he is more interested in the anatomy of the B1.

and with this injection of funds the line was completed and a limited service introduced, between the top of the inclines at either end, from 16th December 1831. Passenger carriages reputedly consisted of old stagecoach bodies on trucks and the journey took about an hour and a quarter, horses drawing the trains along the level sections. The line began operating in its entirety on 3rd April 1832 and an average of over a hundred people a day travelled on the railway that month. Although this may seem a fairly modest level of patronage it is worth noting that a Dundee - Blairgowrie stagecoach two or three times a week had sufficed in 1830. Some 250 passengers used the Dundee & Newtyle on weekdays in July 1835, far exceeding expectations, and the amount of goods traffic was much as predicted. The company was delighted with its own success, though unfortunately this did not translate into profits. As will be seen later, operating costs were excessive and the basic concept of the line was flawed.

A gauge of four feet six and a half inches was adopted for the Newtyle railway and track consisted of lightweight fish-bellied rails laid on stone sleeper blocks. Immediately beyond Ward Road terminus in Dundee the line climbed the eastern slope of the Law by a 1 in 10 incline extending for 1,060 yards. This had single track at the bottom, double track in the middle and three rails at the top, and was operated by a 40hp high pressure stationary engine. Immediately afterwards came Law Tunnel, 330 yards long, then a stopping place (rather than a station) rejoicing in the name of Offset at the Back of Law. A level stretch through the Sidlaw foothills extending for nearly four and three quarter miles followed, and this included primitive stations at Baldovan and Baldragon. At the head of Strathmartine the line climbed Balbeuchly Incline, 1 in 25 for 1,700 yards, and single track throughout. It was worked by a 20hp condensing engine and had a stopping place at the bottom and a station at the top. By now the railway had climbed to 530 feet above sea level, from 330ft at the top of Law Incline and 85 ft at Ward Road. Another four and three quarter mile level section took the track past Auchterhouse station, across Pitnappie Moss in a moderately elevated part of the Sidlaw Hills, and down to Strathmore, by means of Hatton Incline (Chapter 4).

Liff station on 3rd January 1961, almost exactly six years after it closed. This was one of six crossing places on the Dundee - Newtyle line, thus the two platforms. A substantial Caley signal box put the meagre passenger facilities to shame, whilst the large linoleum factory in the background had its own siding.

Thirty-odd years ago, isolated and under-used buildings were not usually subjected to the attention of vandals and arsonists. Despite closing to passengers in 1917, Lochee West station (Victoria then Camperdown in earlier days) was still largely intact on the wet afternoon of 3rd January 1961. Partial stripping away of the canopy had revealed exquisite cast iron brackets, and a bargeboard with clover leaf fretwork added style to this tall timber structure. It once served a district of mills and workers' tenements.

Right. **Ex-Caledonian Pickersgill 4-4-0 No 54500 looked in fine fettle as it stood at Lochee with the SLS Angus Railtour on 20th May 1961. The main building here was solidly constructed of stone rubble and was overlooked by a fine signal box, tall enough to give good visibility round the curve. Note the wooden footbridge, typical of many small Caley stations.**

Abandoned Baldovan station, looking towards Dundee, on 3rd January 1961. This was on the southernmost level section of the 1831 alignment and the stone-faced platform dated from that time. The sagging timber shed could have been a Dundee & Newtyle original, although it was probably a later addition. A timber Caley footbridge can be seen in the distance. This area is now dominated by housing estates.

Baldragon station, viewed here on 3rd January 1961, stood in a remote spot with only farmsteads such as Tyle Cott and North Auchray for company. The sharp curve was typical of the Dundee & Newtyle's level stretch between Law and Balbeuchley inclines. A hipped slate roof and oversized yet simple brackets enhanced the neat timber building.

Newtyle was a remote place - even the village did not then exist - so extensions to Glamis and Coupar Angus were opened in 1837 to reduce cartage (Chapter 4 again). At the Dundee end, a line to the docks became imperative and this was built by a group of shareholders who called themselves 'The Trustees of the Harbour Branch Railway'. It was constructed without an Act of Parliament, but with full approval of the Town Council. The line ran along Lindsay Street, across Nethergate and through a goods warehouse owned by the Trustees, before turning eastwards along Yeaman Shore Road before terminating on the west quay of Earl Grey Dock. Goods traffic began in February 1837 and was worked by horses. Gradients of 1 in 24 and 1 in 37 meant that trips were limited to two wagons at a time.

Increasing traffic on the Dundee & Newtyle itself justified the use of steam locomotives by 1833, so two 0-2-4s (one for each level section) were ordered from Carmichael's Ward Foundry in the town. No 1 EARL OF AIRLIE and No 2 LORD WHARNCLIFFE entered service in September of that year. They had two vertical cylinders, one on either side of the boiler and pioneered the use of a trailing bogie. No 3 TROTTER, a smaller but basically similar engine, was delivered from James Stirling of Dundee in 1834, and No 4 JOHN BULL, a Robert Stephenson 0-4-0, arrived during 1836. Passenger trains now romped along the level stretches at 25mph, although the overall speed was still only 9mph because of the inclines. Local people were fascinated by the 'iron horses' and the oft-quoted scorn of an old Arbroath fisherman who had made the journey especially to see them is worth repeating. 'It's a humbug, a perfect humbug. It puffed a', it puffed a', it cam', an' it cam', and when it saw me it ran into a hole i' the hull an' hoded itsel.' (It puffed, it puffed, it came and it came, and when it saw me it ran into a hole in the hill and hid itself). What he saw from his perch on Dundee Law, of course, was the train entering Law Tunnel!

By 1840 the Dundee & Newtyle had about 170 goods wagons, many without springs, busily engaged in carrying coal, potatoes, flax, yarn and numerous other commodities. There was also a fleet of well-used first class and 'mixed' passenger carriages, most of which still resembled stagecoaches. However, the company could not rid itself of the debt incurred by raising extra revenue during construction

The signal box and stage for exchanging single line tokens were still delightful features of Rosemill loop as late as 3rd January 1961. There was a quarry siding here at one time. Latterly, Ninewells Junction to Newtyle was worked by the electric token block system with crossing places at Liff, Lochee, Fairmuir Junction, Rosemill, Auchterhouse and Newtyle. The brick building on the right was probably a Dundee & Newtyle original.

The simple arched roof and sturdy side walls of Dundee East station dominated D30 4-4-0 No 62434 KETTLEDRUMMLE as it awaited departure with the 1.08pm to Forfar via the direct line on 18th December 1954. Gas lamps did little to brighten up the gloomy interior at night.

and despite the extensions to Glamis and Coupar Angus, developments in Strathmore were sluggish. Furthermore, Dundee had become less dependent on its hinterland, and two thirds of railway goods traffic was northbound, involving costly lifts up two of the inclines. Even passenger services over the eleven mile line involved five engines, three of them stationary. Working expenses absorbed 83 per cent of revenue, compared with 57 per cent on the Garnkirk & Glasgow, and the proprietors despaired. The shareholders had still not received a dividend by 1844 and during that year the railway was advertised for lease. On 27th July 1846 the youthful Dundee & Perth company took up the offer, with effect from the following October. In fairly rapid succession this arrangement was inherited by the Dundee, Perth & Aberdeen, Scottish Central and Caledonian as a result of company expansion and takeovers.

These successive tenants had to address the difficult task of putting the inefficient Dundee & Newtyle into shape and the three inclines were at the top of the agenda. Rope renewal, fuel and staff to run the stationary engines were expensive enough, but compensation for accidents added to the costs. Another familiar anecdote deserves an airing. When the rope parted during a descent of Law Incline in the early days, a farmer's wife using the railway for the first time was thrown off the carriage with her fellow passengers as the train crashed to a halt in Ward Road Station. Surveying her scattered eggs and butter she exclaimed, 'Od, sirs, I liked the ride on the railway, but they hae sic a rough way o' coupin' fouk oot, I dinna think I'll come back by eet.'

The Dundee & Newtyle Improvement Act of 2nd July 1847 authorised gauge conversion and other works, most of which were not carried out for some time. Complete closure for five days during September 1849 was necessary for the transition to standard gauge. Although TROTTER was scrapped, the other three locomotives were converted to run on the widened metals, and survived until 1854 when newer engines from the leasing company were brought in. The Newtyle line carried on much as before, but an Improvement

C16 4-4-2T No 67493 waiting at Dundee East with the 12.19pm suburban working to Barnhill on 8th January 1955. This was the last day of services over the Forfar direct line. Although the local train consisted of two late LMS non-corridors, there was a rake of early LMS compartment stock in one of the bays and LNER Thompson main line coaches were stabled in the other principal platform.

Bright winter sunshine cheered up Dundee East on its last day, 3rd January 1959, just over a year after it had reached its centenary. Camperdown Junction signal box can be seen in the far distance, and the main line to Dock Street tunnel and Tay Bridge station is in a cutting off to the right. Double track in the foreground merged into single track behind the camera and continued through the streets to West Yard, this being the original 1847 connection. The site of Trades Lane passenger terminus was also in the foreground; possibly the platform immediately in front of East station was associated with it. By 1987 the site of Dundee East station had become a car showroom, in a run down area of largely derelict warehouses.

Act of 21st July 1859 heralded great changes. A deviation avoiding Balbeuchly Incline opened on 1st November 1860 incorporating new stations at Dronley and Auchterhouse, the latter replacing original facilities on the abandoned line. Balbeuchly, at the top of the incline also closed (Balbeuchly Foot had disappeared from the timetable in 1855). A more ambitious deviation, completed on 10th June 1861, swept round the western slopes of Dundee Law from Baldovan to the Perth line at Ninewells Junction. New stations were provided at Lochee, Victoria and Liff close to the advancing suburbs, and it meant the end of Law Incline and Ward terminus, together with the northern part of the harbour branch. The enigmatic stopping place at Offset, renamed Cross Roads in the 1840s, seemed to have faded away by 1855.

From the mid-1860s, the Dundee & Newtyle finally achieved stability when, in effect, it became part of the Caledonian system. Local passenger trains and the pick up goods became a familiar part of daily life in the middle of Sidlaws, while the owning company drew rent and paid a modest dividend from its office in Dundee. Apart from those associated with the deviations, the first passenger station to close was Lochee West, on 1st January 1917 (it had been called Victoria until May 1862, then Camperdown to February 1896). The Dundee & Newtyle company was finally wound up on 1st January 1923 when the Caledonian became part of the LMS. After nearly a century and a quarter, passenger services were withdrawn on 10th January 1955 and the line was severed as a through route when goods traffic between Auchterhouse and Newtyle finished, on 5th May 1958. The sidings at Liff, Lochee West and Baldovan closed on 24th February 1964 followed by those at Auchterhouse, Dronley and Baldragon on 25th January 1965. All that remained was the line from Ninewells Junction to Lochee yard and Maryfield goods, at the end of a spur from the erstwhile Fairmuir Junction. When these depots went out of use on 6th

Y9 0-4-0ST No 68110 was in a happy mood, judging by the chalked face on its smokebox, as it trundled through the streets with wagons from the docks on a glorious summer day in the mid-1950s. The ornate Merchant Navy Establishment on the right provided an interesting contrast to the rather strange 1930s frontage of Dundee East. This vaguely Art Deco facade replaced the original end screen which consisted of a flamboyant display of iron and glass in a radial petal-like pattern. Photograph George Staddon, Neville Stead collection.

A trio of Y9 0-4-0ST dock shunters, Nos 68100, 68108 and 68114 at Dundee Harbour on 8th January 1955. Note the spark arrestors, one of several requirements for working over the dock lines. 'Small and light' locomotives approved by the Harbour Engineer had to be employed, speed was not to exceed 4 mph, a mixture of coal and coke had to be burned, and whistles were only to be used when absolutely necessary.

November 1967 the ancient Dundee & Newtyle finally expired.

DUNDEE & ARBROATH

Another early Tayside railway followed the shoreline from Dundee to Arbroath, and in its own way, was also something of a local pioneer. The passage was an easy one, and in marked contrast to the Newtyle branch, no engineering works of note were required. Furthermore, rather than finishing up as a rural backwater, the line showed signs of becoming a trunk route less than thirty years after the first trains ran. Better communication between Dundee, Arbroath and Montrose was an important local issue in the mid-1830s. There was also a fear that the Dundee & Newtyle might become a springing point for a line from these harbours to Perth via Strathmore, thus bypassing Dundee. Lord Panmure, a charismatic Angus landowner, convened a meeting during October 1835 to galvanise interest in a railway and his zealous approach eventually proved successful despite an initial dearth of financial support. The Dundee & Arbroath company received its Act of Parliament on 19th May 1836 and Grainger and Miller of Edinburgh were appointed engineers. Somewhat controversially, they adopted a new gauge of 5ft 6in, for the line was seen as a purely local one and integration with a wider network was not envisaged. T-section iron rails were employed and they rested on a mixture of stone blocks and transverse timber sleepers. The almost level double track kept to the coastal plain and was straightforward to build, most of the land having been donated by Lord Panmure. Right hand running was adopted when the fourteen and a half miles between Arbroath and a temporary terminus at Craigie, well to the east of Dundee, opened on 6th October 1838. There was much rejoicing as the first train, consisting of eleven coaches carrying 400 passengers, averaged a creditable 26mph on its return journey from Arbroath. It was hauled by WALLACE, one of three 2-2-2 locomotives with 5ft 6in driving wheels and horizontal cylinders, supplied by Kinmond, Hutton & Steel of Dundee; the others were FURY and GRIFFIN.

From Craigie the Dundee & Arbroath kept to the shore for a while before running some way inland behind the bulge of coast at Broughty Castle. At Barnhill the line returned to the sea, bridged the

With the dock estate to the right, C16 4-4-2T No 67484 rolled steadily towards Dundee East with the 1.30pm local from Arbroath, on 30th November 1957. Long-closed Stannergate station near the site of the original Dundee & Arbroath Craigie terminus was about half a mile away in the distance.

North British Loco type 2 No D6103 passes fishermen's huts near West Ferry on 25th June 1966 with the lightweight 12.35 Glasgow Buchanan Street to Arbroath. This was a summer Saturday working.

On the warm but dull afternoon of 21st June 1958 C16 4-4-2T No 67501 drifted into West Ferry with the 11.52am from Arbroath to Dundee East. This fair sized station with its more than ample platform canopy was opened by the Dundee & Arbroath Railway in 1859 to serve a growing residential area. A number of villas can be seen in the background. West Ferry closed in 1967 and little trace remains.

mouth of Dighty Water, then ran alongside Monifieth Sands. Beyond Monifieth the tracks headed for Carnoustie and Arbroath, encountering low dunes, several little streams and a gorgeous coastline of rocks and beaches (Chapter 2). Horse buses provided connections to and from Dundee until an extension of a mile and a half as far as Roodyards (also known as Carolina Port) opened on 3rd June 1839. Sceptics doubted whether the railway would be able to compete with road carts and coastal shipping, but it proved a considerable success and carriers soon concentrated on serving the railheads at Broughty Ferry, Monifieth, Carnoustie and East Haven rather than running along the parallel highway. Passenger trains consisted of five carriages which were named after stagecoaches, ANTIQUARY, DOLPHIN and MUCKLEBACKET for example. However, the ride was extremely bumpy and it has been said that some passengers were convinced that the train had left the rails! Three more engines, RAPID, DART and QUEEN arrived from the same Dundee foundry in 1839-41.

On 2nd April 1840 a further extension, this time of three quarters of a mile, opened between Roodyards station (which then closed) and Trades Lane near the docks in Dundee. It was a curious stretch of line. Although the Trades Lane & Carolina Port Railway was built, owned and controlled by the Trustees of Dundee Harbour, as stipulated in the original Dundee & Arbroath Act, it was leased to the main company from the outset. Nevertheless it remained the property of the port authority for nearly seventy years and as such eventually became an integral if tiny part of the East Coast main line. Trades Lane terminus was adjacent to the north side of Victoria Dock and consisted of a wooden shed 320ft long by 30ft wide covering two tracks. Its lack of even the most basic amenities such as waiting rooms immediately gave rise to acrimonious criticism from shareholders and passengers alike. The Dundee & Arbroath carried on in a world of its own for several years; there was no attempt to link it with the Newtyle line for example. However, the explosion of railway promotion in 1845 inevitably drew the local concern into the national network. On the opposite side of Dundee a line was authorised from Perth

Although Broughty Ferry was one of the original Dundee & Arbroath stations dating from 1838, most of it was rebuilt during joint ownership, probably around the turn of the century. By the look of the canopies, North British architects seem to have been responsible. C16 4-4-2T No 67486 paused there on 21st June 1958 with the 12.41pm from Dundee East to Arbroath. The original building, one of the earliest surviving station structures in Scotland, was behind the camera.

Ex-Caledonian Railway 4-2-2 No 123 at Broughty Ferry with the SLS Angus railtour just before its return to Glasgow Queen Street on 20th May 1961. The ample canopies of the rebuilt station are well shown in this view. Note the level crossing gates and the footbridge incorporating a signal box. Proposed replacement by automatic barriers has been a bone of contention with the local council for several years.

Monifieth was also served by Dundee & Arbroath trains from the outset, but again the station underwent reconstruction at a later date, probably during the 1890s in this case. The new buildings were on a massive scale for what was essentially a suburb of Dundee, and Caledonian practice seems to have influenced the design. C16 4-4-2T No 67491 paused at Monifieth with the 12.50pm Dundee East - Carnoustie on 21st June 1958. Some thirty years later parts of the station buildings were reconstructed at Birkhill on the Bo'ness & Kinneil Railway having been rendered redundant by bus shelters.

(see next section) and on 30th April 1847, a month before its own tracks were completed, the Dundee & Perth company began working the Arbroath route. During July and August 1847, the Dundee & Arbroath was converted to standard gauge and conventional left hand running commenced. At the same time a connecting line was laid through the streets from Trades Lane to Dundee West. Although a leasing arrangement was sanctioned in 1848, this was not put into effect and the Arbroath company began running its own line again on 9th March 1850.

As traffic built up it became clear that something had to be done about the shameful affair at Trades Lane. An Act of 3rd July 1851 sanctioned a new station, Dundee East, which opened on 14th December 1857 immediately to the north of the old facilities. It had two lengthy island platforms, the inner ends of which were covered by an arched overall roof 200ft long and 56ft wide. The terminus, together with the approach from Camperdown Junction, were Dundee & Arbroath property - but trains still had to use Harbour Trustees tracks from Carolina Port to reach it. Trades Lane station was removed the following January, although the rails remained part of the route through the streets to Dundee West. This was worked by horses hauling a maximum of three passenger carriages or four wagons at a time. With residential traffic increasing, a station opened at West Ferry during 1859.

The Dundee & Arbroath was vested in the Scottish North Eastern Railway on 31st January 1862 and finally wound up on 28th July 1863. It handed nine engines over to the larger company, although none of these were the originals mentioned earlier. On 10th August 1866 the Scottish North Eastern merged with the Caledonian and the Arbroath line became part of its rapidly expanding system. However, the North British exercised running pow-

The splendid exterior of Dundee West on 1st May 1965, the last day of services. Note the line of rails in the street. These once connected West goods yard with East station and the main docks, whilst a branch can be seen veering off left towards Earl Grey Dock. The original Dundee & Newtyle harbour branch also pursued this course. At the time this interesting corner of the city was alive with activity, including a nervous young lady learning to drive in a new Ford Cortina! Today the scene consists entirely of traffic pouring along one of the Tay road bridge approaches.

Ex-LMS Compound 4-4-0 No 40938, the station pilot, with a rake of non-corridor stock in Dundee West carriage sidings on 31st December 1955. This was a Perth duty, the engine returning home on the 6.10pm passenger train. A corner of the mineral yard can be seen to the left of the tender.

As a Perth Compound on station pilot duties stood in platform 1, ex-Caledonian Pickersgill '72' class 4-4-0 No 54494 made a rather smoky departure from Dundee West with a local working to Perth during the mid-1950s. In true Caley tradition, even the platform lamps had a certain style about them. Photograph George Staddon, Neville Stead collection.

ers and operated two trains a day from Burntisland to Aberdeen via the estuary crossing at Broughty Ferry (see Chapter 9) using its own locomotives. With the Tay Bridge and a connecting line to Camperdown Junction open for traffic, North British agitation led to an Act of 21st July 1879 granting joint ownership of the Dundee to Arbroath section, but before this became effective (on 1st February 1880) the high girders had fallen. During February and March 1880 a station called Camperdown Junction appeared in *Bradshaw,* but it had no trains and was probably never built. Following the reopening of the Tay Bridge in 1887 and the completion of the Forth Bridge in 1890, through expresses from London to Aberdeen began to use the once isolated Dundee & Arbroath tracks. A large suburban station called Stannergate opened just west of the long-abandoned temporary terminus at Craigie in February 1901, but it was no match for the newly electrified street tramways and closed on 1st May 1916. Back in 1894 a suburban railway from the Newtyle line east of Lochee to the Arbroath route at Camperdown Junction was proposed. This would have followed a semi-circular course through Smithfield and Maryfield, but had it ever been built the trams would no doubt have seen it off fairly quickly!

That odd anachronism, the Trades Lane & Carolina Port Railway, finally became part of the joint line on 28th August 1907. At the time the Dundee & Arbroath had its own management based in Dundee, but from 1910 the Caledonian and North British supervised matters from an office in Edinburgh. With the grouping of 1923 this arrangement continued under LMS and LNER control, until nationalisation in 1948. Since then there has been a considerable decline in freight and local passenger services. Stannergate goods yard, which incorporated a siding from the original Craigie terminus, closed on 5th October 1964, followed by the facilities at Dundee East and Monifieth on 2nd January 1967 and 28th April 1969, respectively, also Broughty Ferry, although special sidings remained for some years. West Ferry, with no goods facilities, closed completely on 4th September 1967. However, the most notable casualty was Dundee East passenger terminus itself. The station closed on 5th January 1959 when a revised local service from Perth to Dundee was introduced. W.A.C. Smith visited it on the last day. *'A final trip on 3rd Janu-*

With its days numbered and its departure board long shorn of all local services, Dundee West looked rather empty on 27th April 1963 as Standard class 5 4-6-0 No 73146 awaited departure with the 2.00pm for Glasgow Buchanan Street. Most steam locos were decidedly grimy by this time, although the maroon main line corridor stock was kept smart. By the mid-1980s an industrial estate had been built on the site of the platforms at Dundee West.

On 20th September 1958 J37 0-6-0 No 64619 pulls out of Dundee West yard with a transfer freight. The ex-Caledonian main line is in the foreground whilst Tay Bridge shed coaling plant is in the right background.

ary 1959 from the gloomy, barn-like, gaslit terminus was made on that chill winter evening by the 5.10pm Arbroath local which consisted of Kittybrewster BI No 61343 tender first on four sparsely filled non-corridor coaches. We joined the main line at Camperdown Junction, rattled past dockside factories and the long derelict platforms at Stannergate to deserted West Ferry, reaching Broughty Ferry at 5.19pm. The return journey to Tay Bridge station was made at 5.23pm by an Aberdeen - Edinburgh Waverley train comprising a corridor set including a restaurant car headed by A4 No 60011 EMPIRE OF INDIA.'

As part of a main line, the Dundee & Arbroath has seen top rate motive power for over a century, including Gresley Pacifics from the 1930s to the 1960s. In 1995 InterCity 125s from London King's Cross, Leeds and Plymouth to Aberdeen used the route and frequent services from Glasgow and Edinburgh to Aberdeen linked Dundee with Arbroath. However, ScotRail has virtually abandoned Dundee's suburbs; in 1997Broughty Ferry had just three eastbound and two westbound departures on weekdays, with Monifieth seeing one less in each direction, while Balmassie, Golf Street and Barry Links have been reduced to one train each way.

Departures from Dundee East, Monday to Friday summer 1948

5.30am Carnoustie
6.05am Arbroath
7.20am Arbroath
7.55am Arbroath
8.30am Kingennie
8.55am Arbroath
9.20am Forfar
9.55am Arbroath
12.00 noon Barnhill
12.14pm Carnoustie
12.30pm Arbroath
12.45pm Carnoustie
1.08pm Kingennie
1.27pm Carnoustie
2.10pm Arbroath
3.10pm Arbroath
4.18pm Arbroath
4.23pm Forfar
5.10pm Arbroath
5.34pm Barnhill
5.43pm Carnoustie
5.50pm Forfar
6.10pm Arbroath
6.17pm Barnhill
6.50pm Arbroath
8.25pm Arbroath
9.20pm Arbroath
10.15pm Arbroath

DUNDEE & PERTH

Railway communication between Dundee and Perth, although an obvious link, came some years after the other two local lines on the north side of the Tay. A scheme had been mooted in the 1830s but it failed at an early stage because of awkward landowners. Even when it was eventually

B1 4-6-0 No 61172 approaching Ninewells Junction with a short freight from Dundee to Perth on 27th April 1963. A connection from the down to up track, provided for Newtyle line trains, can just be seen to the left of the engine. The girder span beyond the signal post carried the A82 Dundee - Perth road, whilst the unmistakable Tay Bridge is just visible in the distance.

As the distant Braes of the Carse brooded under a leaden sky, Caprotti Standard 5MT 4-6-0 No 73145 passed Ninewells Junction with the 1.15pm Glasgow Buchanan Street - Dundee West, on 27th April 1963. The Newtyle branch (truncated by this time) came in from the right opposite the signal box. There was a station here for a short time during the 1860s.

Class 5 4-6-0 No 44925 runs into Invergowrie with the 12.30pm local from Dundee West to Perth on 3rd January 1959. On the distant hillside the Newtyle line can be seen climbing away from Ninewells Junction on an embankment. Closure of Invergowrie station was proposed in 1984, but the notice was withdrawn when Tayside Regional Council agreed to subsidise the service. The goods yard in the background finished during 1967.

built, the route remained isolated for a while from the main line at Perth. However, in later years it was furnished with a very handsome terminus at Dundee, and this has often been described as the finest station building in Scotland. The Dundee & Perth Railway acquired its Act of Parliament on 25th May 1845, at the height of the Railway Mania. A gauge of 5ft 6in was contemplated at first but this was changed to standard before construction began, no doubt to conform with the lines all the way from Carlisle to Aberdeen, authorised a couple of months later. Work proceeded rapidly along the mostly flat Carse of Gowrie and passenger services from Dundee Union Street to Barnhill (across the Tay from Perth - see Chapter 9) began on 24th May 1847. The twenty mile line included long level sections with the steepest gradient an easy 1 in 220, whilst curves were frequent but gentle. As a bonus, locomotives had become quite sophisticated by this time and the Dundee & Perth purchased a batch of outside cylinder engines, probably built by Kinmond, Hutton & Steel of Dundee under licence from Hawthorn of Newcastle. The railway clearly fulfilled a pressing need and traffic built up rapidly. Road coaches and river steamers were outclassed, while traders forwarded cargoes from Dundee by rail, thus affecting Perth harbour.

From Dundee the line headed west along the shore overlooking extensive tidal flats, notably My Lord's Bank. A curve round the prominent bay below Ninewells brought the railway to Invergowrie station and beyond here it followed the coast for a short distance to Kingoodie. The tracks then ventured further and further inland across the Carse of Gowrie at elevations varying from 20 to 50 feet above sea level, passing farmsteads such as Clatteringbrigs and Waterybutts as well as the wayside stations of Longforgan and Inchture. Away to the north the Braes of Carse, the southern flank of the Sidlaw Hills, rise abruptly to over 900 ft. Ahead lay Errol and the rather more constricted approach to Perth (Chapter 6). Three branches were associated with the Dundee & Perth. The first was the connection across Dundee, built at the expense of the Harbour Trustees and noted earlier. A high level viaduct line along a similar course was sanctioned by the Act of 22nd July 1848, but this was never built. The second branch was marvellously eccentric. Lord Kinnaird, although the first Dundee

The Inchture Village tram, resplendent in Caledonian livery, during the winter of 1905. Its terminus in the background largely consisted of stables - one of the lesser known motive power depots in Scotland! The building was more or less in original condition seventy years after the passenger service was withdrawn. Photograph Perth and Kinross District Council, Museums and Art Galleries.

Class 5 4-6-0 No 44879 on arrival at Dundee Tay Bridge with the 10.45 from Blackpool North on 9th July 1966. The summer Saturday train had reached its destination at 18.53, some 56 minutes late. In this view the curved platform, hefty canopy and massive retaining walls are well shown.

Pacifics at Dundee Tay Bridge on 4th July 1959. Class A2/1 No 60509 WAVERLEY, in charge of the 5.17pm Aberdeen - Edinburgh Waverley, takes water as A3 No 60087 BLENHEIM stands on the adjoining through line. High tide is approximately level with the running plates of the engines.

& Perth chairman, was not keen to have the railway close to his seat at Rossie Priory, north of Inchture. Consequently it pursued a course two miles south of the village. However, a line to Inchture itself opened in 1848 and this was operated by a horse-drawn dandy with the occasional steam special venturing further afield. The third feeder appeared during 1861 in the form of the Lochee deviation of the Dundee & Newtyle. A station was provided at Ninewells Junction, although it soon closed - probably in October 1865.

As described earlier, the infant Dundee & Perth leased the Dundee & Newtyle in 1846, but was itself wooed by the equally youthful Scottish Central during 1847 as a means of blocking the rival Edinburgh & Northern. Developments came thick and fast in the wake of the Mania! Nevertheless, the Perth company remained independent and changed its name to the somewhat pretentious Dundee, Perth & Aberdeen Junction Railway in 1848 as a result of its interests in the Arbroath line. It was finally vested in the Scottish Central on 28th July 1863 and thus became part of the Caledonian on 5th July 1865. Magdalen Green station opened in 1878 to serve a suburb of Dundee, but a much more spectacular improvement came eleven years later. The original terminus at Union Street had been rebuilt during 1862 with a modest classical facade featuring a two storey central block incorporating balustrades, a little pediment and a pleasant clock tower. The station was renamed Dundee West during October 1866. However, the Caledonian was eager to make more of an impact in Dundee following the vastly enhanced North British presence as a result of the Tay Bridge. The result was one of the most beautifully proportioned late Victorian railway buildings in Britain and a celebration of Scottish Baronial architecture.

Opened in 1889, the new Dundee West was constructed of sandstone and had an eight bay, two storey facade with Tudor windows. A steep pitched roof was punctuated by six little dormers and two prominent stepped gables, one sprouting a chimney at the apex and the other flanked by projecting turrets. A bulky yet very elegant tower at the southern end dominated the station; it, too, had round corner turrets finished off with conical spires, whilst the roof was extremely steep and reminiscent of a French chateau. The cab rank was sheltered by a delicate iron and glass canopy. Inside there was a lofty booking hall with a semi-circular ticket office facing the entrance, and telegraph and parcels offices either side. Beyond the

Gresley A4 Pacific No 60023 GOLDEN EAGLE drifting down into Dundee Tay Bridge with the 10.30am Edinburgh Waverley to Aberdeen on 8th August 1964. The train consisted of a motley collection of Gresley, Thompson, Stanier and BR Standard main line corridor stock.

V2 2-6-2 No 60813, unique among the class in being fitted with a stovepipe chimney and a small semi-circular smoke deflector, runs into Dundee Tay Bridge with the 14.25 from Edinburgh Waverley on 20th August 1966. A southbound express has just departed. Note the two bay platforms and the constricted approach between former North British and Caledonian goods yards, on the left and right respectively.

generous concourse were two main platforms, each with their own side bay. A large overall roof formed of transverse gables culminating in clerestories covered much of the station and sheltered a bookstall, confectionery cabin and waiting rooms, together with first and third class refreshment facilities.

In its heyday the station had an impressive timetable. During 1922 for example, there were through trains to Glasgow, Edinburgh, Manchester, Liverpool, the west of England and London Euston (including sleepers). Local services ran to Perth, Gleneagles, Crieff and Blairgowrie, whilst a substantial amount of residential traffic had developed over the years. At the time there were about 90 staff, including no less than 42 porters. A goods depot occupied ten acres immediately south of the passenger station and this incorporated a massive warehouse dealing inevitably with jute and jam amongst a myriad of commodities. The yard could accommodate 750 wagons at a time and handled up to 15,000 tons of mineral traffic alone each month. Some 170 people were employed by the goods side. Just under half a mile from the terminus an eight road engine shed stood on the north side of the running lines.

Class J39 0-6-0 No 64792 departs from Dundee Tay Bridge with the 5.25pm local to St Andrews on 20th September 1958. With a burnt smokebox door and leaking cylinder glands, the engine looked in need of some attention. The huge North British warehouse forms a backdrop.

Retrenchment began, hardly surprisingly, with the closure of the Inchture Village line on 1st January 1917. From 1895 the horses hauled a specially built single deck tramcar painted in standard Caledonian colours, but by Edwardian times the branch had already become a curiosity. Just under forty years later the local service from Dundee to Perth was rationalised with the closure of Magdalen Green, Longforgan and Inchture stations, on 11th June 1956. Inchture yard on the main line (Inchture Village never handled goods) finished on 2nd November 1964, followed by the facilities at Longforgan and Invergowrie on 25th January 1965 and 14th August 1967 respectively. Dundee West, having lost its Blairgowrie trains in 1955, was further emasculated when the local service from Perth began to use Tay Bridge station via the spur at Buckingham Junction in 1959. This left half a dozen workings a day to Glasgow Buchanan Street and there were long periods of slumber. The end came on 3rd May 1965 when these trains were diverted

On 30th November 1957, V2 2-6-2 No 60888 in charge of the 10.00am Edinburgh Waverley to Aberdeen express emerges from the cutting east of Dock Street tunnel, on the climb out of Dundee Tay Bridge. The train is about to pass Camperdown Junction where double track veered off to East station on the right and a single line headed towards the harbour lines to the left.

With the former Caledonian loco shed on the right and the westernmost sidings of Tay Bridge yard on the left, B1 4-6-0 No 61261 led empty stock from the 12.35 Glasgow Buchanan Street - Kirkcaldy down the Tay Bridge approach viaduct on Saturday 20th August 1966. The coaches, worked forward from Kirkcaldy by a Thornton engine, then formed the Sunday 14.55 from Dundee to Glasgow. Note the former Esplanade station beyond the train.

On 1st May 1965 V2 2-6-2 No 60824 climbs towards the Tay Bridge with the lengthy Dundee, Perth & London Shipping Company freight. By this time the firm had ceased operating coasters, although the replacement charter train did not last long either.

to Tay Bridge station as well. Sadly, and very much to the detriment of Dundee, West station was demolished shortly afterwards to make way for one of the Tay road bridge approaches. Goods facilities at West yard, ultimately a Freightliner terminal, survived until 4th March 1988. The old Caledonian shed, latterly a diesel multiple unit depot, closed in October 1981. In 1995 the Dundee & Perth line had sixteen eastbound and eighteen westbound trains on weekdays, most of them workings between Glasgow and Aberdeen. Invergowrie, the last suburban station on the west side of Dundee, had just three services each way.

Departures from Dundee West, Monday to Friday summer 1948

6.55am Perth
7.52am Glasgow Buchanan Street
9.00am Perth
10.45am Perth
11.35am Glasgow Buchanan Street (restaurant car)
12.00 noon Blairgowrie
12.45pm Perth
3.00pm Glasgow Buchanan Street
4.10pm Perth
4.20pm Blairgowrie/Alyth
4.40pm Glasgow Buchanan Street
5.10pm Perth
5.40pm Blairgowrie
6.10pm Perth
7.15pm Glasgow Buchanan Street
8.50pm Perth
10.00pm Perth

DUNDEE TAY BRIDGE

The first Tay Bridge placed Dundee on a main line to the north and gave the city a new through station. It also established the North British as the principal east coast route, especially as plans for the Forth Bridge were well advanced. Despite the awful disaster of December 1879, there was a proven need for the direct Edinburgh - Dundee - Aberdeen line and the bridge was, of course, rebuilt. Eventually through coaches from Penzance to Aberdeen were to be seen at Tay Bridge station, whilst villages in Fife became sizeable dormitory suburbs of Dundee. The bridge itself is the main subject of Chapter 9, leaving this section to deal with associated lines actually in the city.

After much debate and a couple of unsuccessful schemes, the Tay Bridge and its connecting lines were sanctioned by an Act of 15th July 1870. Regular traffic began on 1st June 1878. Following the collapse of the high girders on 28th December 1879, passenger services from Burntisland to Tay Bridge station re-

B1 4-6-0s Nos 61278 and 61172 waiting to depart from Tay Bridge yard with the 12.10pm Dundee, Perth & London Shipping Company freight on 24th July 1965. The train was normally powered by a V2, but these were required for passenger work as this was the start of the Dundee Trades Holiday. Class J37 0-6-0 No 64608 is the yard pilot.

Class V2 2-6-2 No 60818 leaving Dundee with southbound cement empties from Aberdeen on 14th August 1965. Tay Bridge shed is on the left.

Despite their mantle of grime, J37 0-6-0 No 64600, B1 4-6-0 No 61263 and J38 0-6-0 No 65931 looked cheerful in the bright sunshine as they stood alongside the coaling plant at Tay Bridge shed on 20th May 1961. As with many depots, ash threatened to bury the rails and an ancient coach in departmental guise lurked in a corner. The Tay Bridge main line is off to the left and the tracks out of Dundee West away to the right.

verted to the Broughty Ferry crossing (Chapter 9) and freight used the Caledonian from Perth. The new bridge was officially opened on 13th June 1887 with public trains commencing a week later. From the curved northern end of the bridge a brick viaduct descended at 1 in 66 towards Tay Bridge station. Esplanade station stood high on the viaduct, close to the end of the bridge, whilst a trailing connection from Buckingham Junction on the Perth - Dundee line came in where the North British tracks reached ground level. By Tay Bridge station the line was a few feet below sea level and massive stone retaining walls rose up either side. Immediately east of the station was Dock Street tunnel (628 yards) which had pumps working all the time to prevent flooding. Beyond here a gradient of 1 in 60, also in a stone lined cutting, lifted trains up to Camperdown Junction on the Dundee - Arbroath route. The distance from the end of the Tay Bridge to Camperdown Junction was just under a mile and a half.

Large, robust, yet architecturally undistinguished, Tay Bridge station was basically a broad island platform 476 yards long and quite severely curved at its eastern end. The up and down main lines ran along either side, but at the western end two bays were provided for Fife locals. Through goods tracks flanked the platform roads immediately below the severe retaining walls. A wide canopy, consisting of transverse glazed gables supported by hefty columns and big spandrels with minimal decoration, sheltered most of the passenger area. This generous roof also masked the station buildings, all of which were at platform level. A stairway from South Union Street led to the first block which included the booking office and stationmaster's accommodation. The second block was occupied by sundry rooms and luggage hoists. The third block incorporated refreshment and dining rooms, waiting accommodation and the telegraph office. It also featured a large projecting clock. A fourth building housed staff and waiting rooms with the offices of the Northern District Commercial Superintendent above. Although access was principally from South Union Street, three pedestrian bridges (to the parcels office, platform and Superintendent's office respectively) spanned the up tracks from a road to the goods yard. In later North British years the station issued almost 300,000 tickets annually and more than 150 staff were under the control of the stationmaster.

Passenger trains throughout the steam era were very varied. For example, in 1922 the principal northbound services including a King's Cross - Aberdeen sleeper with through coaches from Penzance, another sleeper from King's Cross and St Pancras to Aberdeen, a day express from King's Cross and St Pancras to Aberdeen, and

Tay Bridge shed hosted quite a variety of motive power. Nose to nose on 16th June 1960 were K4 2-6-0 No 61996 LORD OF THE ISLES and Standard 5MT 4-6-0 No 73008. The engines were from Thornton and Perth sheds respectively.

two Edinburgh - Aberdeen expresses, one with a through coach to Elgin. There were balancing southbound workings. A frequent service of main line stopping trains linked Dundee with Edinburgh and Glasgow. Apart from one Perth - Arbroath working, eastbound short distance traffic was handled at Dundee East. However, numerous local services to and from Newport, Tayport and St Andrews crossed the Tay Bridge, particularly during the morning, lunchtime and evening peaks. Three signal boxes controlled the North British station, but day to day operations were not always easy. Long southbound trains immediately faced a stiff climb, with the last few coaches still squealing round the sharp curve, and this led to much slipping in wet weather. At the east end, loco changes, shunting and vehicle transfers were only accomplished by venturing into Dock Street tunnel. Being in a dip, the tunnel lacked a good through draught and was often smoke laden, so electric lamp repeaters were employed inside, rather than the mechanical arms elsewhere. Furthermore, despite its size, the station had limited accommodation and on numerous occasions all four platforms could be occupied by trains awaiting departure.

The North British goods facilities extended all the way from South Union Street to Esplanade station, on the south side of the running lines. At the eastern end, the main depot incorporated a warehouse over 400 feet long, twelve hydraulic cranes, and some thirty sidings with a capacity of nearly 400 wagons. At the western end six long sidings extended almost up to Esplanade station. In its heyday the goods station and mineral yard handled almost 9,000 wagons a month carrying over 35,000 tons of traffic, principally raw jute, flax, hemp, hessian, coal, livestock, preserves, confectionery, whisky, groceries, machinery, shipbuilding materials and ships' supplies. There were about 130 staff, plus a dozen harbour shunters. Freights ran north to Montrose, Forfar and Aberdeen, whereas southbound departures were for Leith, Glasgow, Bathgate and Carlisle. Caledonian goods trains and trip workings to and from the docks used the spur at Buckingham Junction and ran through Tay Bridge station. A large amount of Fife coal traffic was also transferred to the Perth line by means of the connection. The six road North British local shed stood immediately north of the running lines.

Esplanade station closed as a wartime economy measure on 1st January 1917, but reopened on 1st February 1919. However, it became a victim of hostilities a second time and closed permanently on 2nd October 1939, immediately prior to being taken over by the War Department. Dundee Tay Bridge loco shed closed on 1st May 1967 with the end of Scottish Region steam, whilst the goods depot lingered on with much reduced activity until 16th May 1983. Various sidings for storage and departmental purposes remained in the mid-1990s. The Harbour branch from Camperdown Junction was still used for oil deliveries and imported paper in April 1981 but finished shortly afterwards. During 1985-86 improvements to track and signalling in the Dundee area costing £2.5 million were carried out, but plans for a rail-bus interchange were abandoned in 1988. Tay Bridge station, now just plain Dundee, has a modern booking office at street level, although it is rather cut off by dual carriageways feeding the Tay road bridge. In summer 1995 a total of eighty passenger trains served the station on weekdays. These included the 'Cornishman' to Penzance - almost like the old days!

Departures from Dundee Tay Bridge, Monday to Friday summer 1948

5.19am Aberdeen (ex London King's Cross) THE ABERDONIAN

5.46am Aberdeen (ex London King's Cross)
5.50am Edinburgh Waverley
6.40am Tayport
7.00am Edinburgh Waverley
7.25am Tayport
7.32am Leuchars Junction
7.51am London King's Cross (ex Aberdeen)
8.40am Edinburgh Waverley
8.47am Tayport
9.07am Perth (via Newburgh)
9.37am Aberdeen (ex Edinburgh Waverley)
9.42am Edinburgh Waverley (ex Montrose)
11.26am London King's Cross (ex Aberdeen)
11.40am Tayport
11.51am Aberdeen (ex Edinburgh Waverley)
12.28pm Edinburgh Waverley (via Tayport)
12.47pm Tayport
1.00pm Tayport
1.46pm Edinburgh Waverley
1.58pm Tayport
2.15pm Edinburgh Waverley (via Tayport and Crail)
2.43pm Edinburgh Waverley (ex Aberdeen)
2.50pm Edinburgh Waverley
4.02pm Aberdeen (ex Edinburgh Waverley)
4.10pm Edinburgh Waverley
4.16pm Tayport
4.45pm Edinburgh Waverley (via Crail)
5.04pm Perth (via Newburgh)
5.15pm Tayport
5.23pm Edinburgh Waverley (ex Aberdeen)
5.25pm Arbroath (local)
5.57pm Tayport
6.20pm Edinburgh Waverley
6.27pm Tayport
6.29pm Aberdeen (ex Edinburgh Waverley)
7.16pm Edinburgh Waverley (ex Aberdeen)
7.35pm Tayport
8.00pm London King's Cross
8.12pm Aberdeen (ex London King's Cross)
8.42pm London King's Cross (ex Aberdeen) THE ABERDONIAN
8.50pm Tayport
9.07pm Edinburgh Waverley (ex Aberdeen)
9.08pm Aberdeen (ex Edinburgh Waverley)
9.50pm Tayport
10.25pm St Andrews
11.00pm Tayport

Allocation at Dundee Tay Bridge shed (62B), summer 1955. (There was no separate allocation at Dundee West shed, which functioned as an annexe to the former LNER shed until it became a diesel depot in 1960).

A2 4-6-2 (2)
V2 2-6-2 (11)
B1 4-6-0 (8)
D30 4-4-0 (2)
D34 4-4-0 (1)
D49 4-4-0 (1)
C16 4-4-2T (7)
J35 0-6-0 (1)
J36 0-6-0 (4)
J37 0-6-0 (8)
J39 0-6-0 (5)
J67 0-6-0T (2)
J83 0-6-0T (7)
Y9 0-4-0ST (5)
WD 2-8-0 (6)
Stanier 4-6-0 (4)
Fairburn 2-6-4T (4)
Standard 2-6-4T (2)
Ivatt 2MT 2-6-0 (2)
Caledonian 0-4-4T (1)
Total 83

On 20th August 1966 A2 Pacific No 60530 SAYAJIRAO was acting as standing pilot at Tay Bridge shed. Also present was J37 No 64608, one of the last ex-North British 0-6-0s eking out a living on local freight workings, including a daily trip to Montrose which lasted until 1967.

Above. A new station was built at Carnoustie in about 1900. It had large timber buildings and wide platforms with a particularly generous canopy on the north side. Most unusually, this had little acanthus leaf decorations at each apex. C16 4-4-2T No 67491 stands at the up platform with the 1.30pm local to Dundee East on 21st June 1958. There is a glimpse of the North Sea just above the engine, but the original stone-built Dundee & Arbroath station house is out of sight behind the camera.

Below. In a view which teases the eye and defies perspective, Fairburn 2-6-4T No 42693 heading the 4.10pm Arbroath to Dundee East stopping train passes West Links station on Kerr's Miniature Railway. This quarter mile long, 10.25 inch gauge holiday line just south of Arbroath was opened alongside the East Coast main line in 1935 (to a gauge three inches smaller) and continues to operate under the auspices of Matthew Kerr Junior. A petrol engined, scaled down version of North British Atlantic No 9872 AULD REEKIE with 'Flying Scotsman' headboard is in the foreground of this 21st June 1958 scene.

Chapter 2

ARBROATH, FORFAR AND CARMYLLIE

ARBROATH ABBEY

North of Dundee the Sidlaws begin to peter away, having made a last defiant stand at Gallow Hill just under 1,250 feet above sea level. Apart from the prominent outcrop of Fotheringham Hill and a swelling at Carmyllie Hill, the ground drops unevenly but relentlessly towards the North Sea at Lunan Bay. A few miles north of this residue of high ground lies Forfar, towards the eastern end of Strathmore. Beyond here this broad vale merges with the valley of the South Esk making its way from the Highlands to Montrose Bay. The coast also changes character east of Dundee. After Carnoustie it begins to swing northwards in a sweeping curve through Arbroath and Montrose, with cliffs overlooking shelves of rock exposed at high tide stretching between broad sandy bays. In the 1830s virtually the whole triangle of land between Dundee, Arbroath and Forfar was highly productive farmland blessed with reserves of good building stone as well. Dundee was a growing industrial town, Arbroath had a flourishing harbour and Forfar was an important agricultural centre with several linen factories. It was clearly logical to link them with railways. The Dundee & Arbroath came early (as seen in Chapter 1) and the Arbroath & Forfar was its contemporary, but the Dundee - Forfar link had to wait for a while. A branch with a varied and unusual career ventured into the centre of the triangle at Carmyllie. Railway history was rarely straightforward however, and two sides of the triangle became embroiled in the drive to establish trunk routes from London to Aberdeen. No less than three terminus stations, built with a firm future in mind, soon became victims of progress.

ARBROATH & FORFAR

There had been a pressing need for better communication between Strathmore and the coast since the late 1700s and canals were proposed on several occasions from 1788 to 1817. In 1835 a railway was seen as the only solution, for the need had become more acute. Timber and peat - traditional fuels for the Angus linen industry - were becoming depleted, and Northumbrian coal imported through Arbroath had to be carted along poor roads at great expense. Increasing amounts of lime for use on the fields were carried in the same way. There was also enormous potential for exporting local stone for use in buildings and pavements in the industrial towns of central Scotland. The Arbroath & Forfar Railway was conceived in 1835, Grainger and Miller surveyed the line, and the Act of Parliament was obtained on 19th May 1836. Local people, together with the town councils at Forfar and Arbroath, were wholly behind the railway, but both the Turnpike Trustees and the occupants of Guthrie Castle caused problems. The former harassed the company for four years and forced a diversion of the main road incorporating two rail overbridges at Friockheim. Difficulties at Guthrie produced a far more interesting solution. The landowner did not wish to see the railway and insisted on a tunnel, which would have been faintly ridiculous in the flat fields, so the Arbroath & Forfar plotted a course further south - but this upset the Turnpike Trustees. Eventually the original route was accepted, providing it crossed the castle driveway by means of an ornamental arch. The Guthrie Gate, an exquisite Tudor creation with turrets, battlements, shields and a coat of arms, was the result.

Otherwise, construction proved straightforward and earthworks were light. Climbing steadily out of Arbroath, the line headed northwards up an attractive little valley past St Vigean's, then north westwards to Letham Grange about 90 feet above sea level. There was a station here for Colliston village, about a mile away on the Turnpike. A further rise to Leysmill (120 feet) led to the Lunan Water valley at Friockheim where the route turned west towards Guthrie at 160 feet. Beyond a delightful stretch alongside Balgavies Loch and Roscobie Loch between prominent Turin Hill to the north and Dunnichen Hill to the south, the track reached Clocksbriggs about 200 feet up. The terminus on the northern edge of Forfar was reached after a gentle south westerly curve. Although the original estimate for the fifteen and a half mile Arbroath & Forfar Railway had been £57,000, it eventually cost £230,000 including rolling stock, which for some reason was left out of the initial calculations. Provision had been made for 5 ft 6 in gauge double track, although only a single line was laid using 66,500 locally quarried stone sleeper blocks and lightweight rails from Northumberland. None of the stations were ready when the line opened, but attractive cottage-like buildings in local stone were eventually provided.

A frugal passenger service from Arbroath Harbour to Leysmill began on 24th November 1838 using a horse-drawn third class carriage, and the remainder of the line to Forfar Playfield opened ten days later on 4th December, with provision for first class passengers. Three 2-2-2 locomotives with 5 ft driving wheels were ordered from Dundee Foundry in November 1837, and when the first of them was finally delivered the company announced that the official public opening of the line, together with a new terminus at Arbroath Catherine Street, would be on 3rd January 1839.

Over 560 people in festive mood travelled behind VICTORIA during the celebrations. Unfortunately the engine broke down two days later and the horses were back for nearly a fortnight. CALEDONIAN was delivered on 15th March and BRITANNIA arrived on 4th May, but the company was chronically short of motive power, coaches and wagons. It was overwhelmed by goods traffic and the pre-

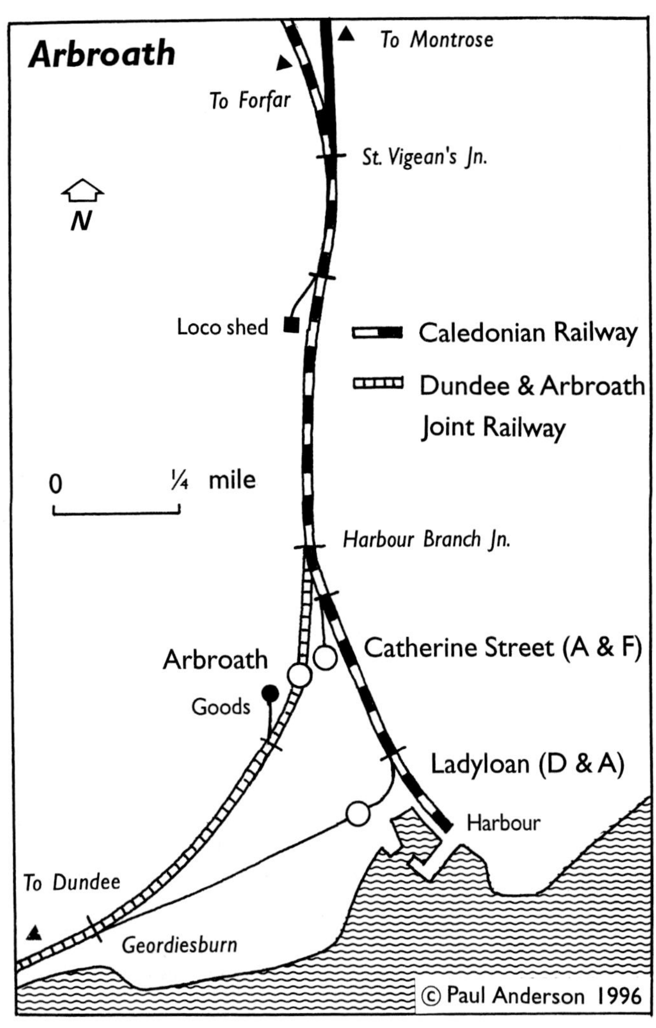

dicted first year total of 60,000 passengers was reached in six months. Previously there had been insufficient demand to support a regular Forfar - Arbroath coach, and the lure of Dundee was completely underestimated. Some relief came when PRINCESS and ALBERT were added to the loco stock. With a lack of signalling, incidents were inevitable. In February 1841 BRITANNIA and VICTORIA collided at Clocksbriggs and were so badly damaged that they had to be sent back to Dundee for repair. Nevertheless the line gained a reputation for success and the drivers, attired in white coats and blue caps with red bands, became the elite of the district.

In Chapter 1 the route of the Dundee & Arbroath Railway was described as far as Monifieth and it is necessary to have a brief look at the eastern section before examining the relationship between the two early lines in Arbroath. Beyond Monifieth the track continued in a straight line across the dunes towards Carnoustie, but it was well inland because of the great bulge of Buddon Ness. This sparsely settled countryside became the preserve of soldiers and golfers and two stations, with complex histories, met their needs. A private halt called Barry Review Platform existed in the early 1890s near Barry Buddon Camp, but it briefly appeared in the public timetable as Buddon from 1910 to 1915, remaining open to receive military specials for another forty or so years. Further on was Barry Links, plain Barry from its opening in 1851 to its renaming in 1919. It was built on the site of a halt called Deyhouse (1843 to 1847) and is still open. The Dundee & Arbroath returned to the coast at Carnoustie which had passenger facilities from the outset, although the platforms were rebuilt on the east side of the level crossing about 1900. During the early 1960s Carnoustie gained its own suburban station, Golf Street Halt, just over half a mile west of the town centre, and it remains open. Continuing eastwards the line encountered the little harbour at East Haven which enjoyed passenger facilities from the opening of the line until 4th September 1967. Sand replaced rock along the shoreline and the village of Elliot, overlooking a broad beach, gained a station in 1855. It became Elliot Junction when the Carmyllie passenger service began, but also closed on 4th September 1967. Beyond here the rails climbed at 1 in 97 for a third of a mile - the only gradient of note all the way from Dundee - then descended towards Arbroath.

The Dundee & Arbroath built quite an impressive station at Lady Loan near Arbroath harbour. It was a long two-storey stone building with dormer windows in the roof and a 'high pitched Gothic roof' covering the platform and two tracks. A single line crossed West Grimsby Street to join Arbroath & Forfar metals in the harbour area and through goods traffic was worked along it by horses. When Catherine Street station opened a coach ran between the two termini. Through fares from Forfar to Dundee were available and the respective timetables were roughly co-ordinated, but this proved an unsatisfactory arrangement and there was constant agitation for a proper link. Eventually the impetus for such an improvement came from way beyond Arbroath. In July 1845, at the height of the Railway Mania, the Scottish Central, Scottish Midland Junction and Aberdeen companies received their Acts of Parliament and by the following September all of them had approached the Arbroath & Forfar with a view to amalgamation. Furthermore, the last two were to have junc-

Ex-Caledonian 0-4-4T No 55230 rolled into Colliston on Saturday 3rd December 1955 with the 1.35pm from Arbroath to Forfar. This was the last day of services and the railwayman wheeling his bike along the platform seemed grimly resigned to the closure. The village was over a mile away to the west and only Letham Grange and farms such as Colliston Castle were in the immediate vicinity. Colliston station had low staggered platforms separated by a level crossing and only the up side remained in use after singling of the line.

At Friockheim the original stone building was later joined by a timber amenities block with a canopy supported on decorative cast iron brackets of generous proportions. Overcoats were necessary on the raw winter afternoon of 3rd December 1955 as ex-Caledonian 0-4-4T No 55230 departed with the 12.30pm from Forfar to Arbroath. The little village of Friockheim was immediately to the right. There were staggered platforms here as well.

tions with the local line (at Forfar and Guthrie respectively) which would thus become part of a trunk route. As described in Chapter 1, the Dundee & Arbroath was destined to become part of the national network as well, and 5ft 6in track was doomed with the spread of standard gauge. The Aberdeen Railway and Scottish Midland Junction Railway will be examined in Chapters 3 and 4. Here it is sufficient to say that the Arbroath & Forfar was leased by the Aberdeen Company from 1st February 1848 when the latter's line between Guthrie and Montrose opened. However, the local concern retained its corporate identity until the grouping of 1st January 1923. Relaying of the Forfar - Arbroath route with standard gauge double track began in 1846 and was finally completed at the southern end in August 1848.

The long-awaited connection at Arbroath was authorised by the Dundee & Arbroath Act of 3rd July 1846. It ran from Geordiesburn, on the approach to Lady Loan, to Amerieclose (later Harbour Branch Junction) just north of Catherine Street and was half a mile long. A substantial cutting at the southern end known as 'the gullet' sliced through the ridge which the original Dundee & Arbroath line had climbed over. Goods traffic commenced on 23rd December 1847 and passenger services began on 1st February 1848, calling at a temporary through station towards the northern end. Catherine Street and Lady Loan closed at the same time, although the latter was still used as a dwelling in the 1950s. The line from Geordiesburn to Lady Loan was abandoned when the link opened. In May 1853 the makeshift joint station was replaced by a permanent structure incorporating a large stone entrance building next to the bridge under Keptie Street. This had a severe classical facade with a heavy cornice and a five bay arcade. Half a century later this station was also regarded as inadequate, so a more spacious affair with generous platform canopies was provided in 1911. At the Forfar end, Playfield was closed to passengers and a new through station opened, when the Scottish Midland Junction route became operational on 2nd August 1848. The original terminus survived as a goods yard at the end of a spur.

In 1883 a line from St Vigean's Junction (north of Arbroath) to Kinnaber Junction (north of Montrose) was completed and this became part of the East Coast main line when the second Tay Bridge opened. As a result the old Arbroath & Forfar virtually became three railways. From Forfar to Guthrie it carried Caledonian expresses to Aberdeen, whilst the short section from Arbroath to St Vigean's Junction was used by fast North British trains to the Grampian coast. The remainder became a docile but valued rural link served by Caley locals and was singled between Guthrie Junction and Letham Mill (near St Vigean's) in 1936. Passenger trains between Forfar and Arbroath were withdrawn on 5th December 1955 and all intermediate stations closed, with the exception of Auldbar Road which survived until 11th June 1956 - presumably in an attempt to retain some custom from the large village of Letham some way to the south. Goods facilities at Guthrie finished on 3rd August 1959, the unstaffed public siding at Clocksbriggs closed on 15th June 1964 and Colliston, Leysmill and Friockheim lost their yards on 25th January 1965, thus making the Guthrie - Letham Mill section redundant (the link from St Vigean's Junction was severed when passenger service ceased). Sidings at Auldbar Road survived until 23rd May 1966. In Arbroath the old harbour branch was retained for fish traffic until 1st November 1963. All expresses between Glasgow and Aberdeen were routed via Dundee from 4th September 1967 and the former Arbroath & Forfar line between Forfar and Guthrie was abandoned. Playfield terminus was retained as a coal depot until 31st October 1979, served by the trip working from Perth. Forfar's main yard closed on 7th June 1982.

Clocksbriggs seen from the 1.35pm from Arbroath to Forfar on 3rd December 1955. This station also had a simple stone building, enhanced by a couple of bay windows and a glass fronted waiting room. Trees forming the backdrop belonged to Reswallie estate, which was quite happy to release a strip of land for the Arbroath & Forfar Railway. Clocksbriggs was the name of a big house, demolished many years before the station closed.

Ex-Caledonian 0-6-0 No 57441 shunting petrol wagons along the branch to the original Arbroath & Forfar Playfield terminus at Forfar on 25th February 1961. The main line was behind the sleeper fence to the right and the passenger station a short distance away.

Departures from Forfar, Monday to Friday, Summer 1948

1.45am Aberdeen (ex-Glasgow Buchanan Street)
6.30am Kirriemuir
6.36am Aberdeen (ex-Glasgow Central)
7.45am Dundee East (direct)
7.53am Glasgow Buchanan Street (ex-Aberdeen)
8.05am Brechin (via Careston)
8.09am Arbroath
8.25am Aberdeen (local ex-Perth)
9.35am Perth (local ex-Arbroath)
10.00am Arbroath
10.09am Aberdeen (ex-Glasgow Buchanan Street)
10.20am Kirriemuir
11.10am Glasgow Buchanan Street (ex-Aberdeen)
11.45am Aberdeen (ex-Glasgow Buchanan Street)
12.23pm Aberdeen (ex-Glasgow Buchanan Street)
12.25pm Kirriemuir
12.30pm Arbroath
2.00pm Blairgowrie (ex-Arbroath)
2.44pm Glasgow Buchanan Street (ex-Aberdeen)
2.45pm Dundee East (direct)
2.52pm Arbroath
4.09pm Aberdeen (ex-Glasgow Buchanan Street)
4.18pm Arbroath
4.40pm Glasgow Buchanan Street (ex-Aberdeen)
5.18pm Kirriemuir
5.23pm Brechin (via Careston)
5.25pm Arbroath
5.40pm Aberdeen
6.15pm Perth (local ex-Aberdeen)
6.50pm Dundee East (direct)
7.05pm Glasgow Buchanan Street (ex-Aberdeen)
7.30pm Aberdeen (ex-Glasgow Buchanan Street)
7.40pm Arbroath

On Saturdays there were 15 additional trains, including three between 10.00pm and 10.30pm.

FORFAR DIRECT

Proposals for a railway between Forfar and Dundee dated back to Scottish North Eastern days, but the roundabout route through Arbroath seemed to satisfy most requirements, particularly after the link was completed. Eventually the Caledonian saw some potential in building a direct route across the Sidlaw foothills which would tap this productive agricultural area. The 17.5 mile single track line from Broughty Ferry Junction to Forfar North Junction opened for goods traffic on 12th August 1870 and passenger services three months later on 14th November. Monikie station opened in 1871.

From Broughty Ferry Junction the branch rose steadily on the coastal side of the Arbroath line then crossed it by means of a plate girder skew bridge. Just beyond here was Barnhill station. It eventually became the starting point for residential services to Dundee and proved the busiest place on the line. The ground then fell away, but the track had to gain height and Dighty Water valley was crossed on a viaduct approached by substantial embankments. The alignment soon changed from north eastwards to north westwards and the climb continued in the shadow of Laws Hill (430 feet), the slopes of which had quarries served by the railway. Kingennie station, just over three miles from the junction at Broughty Ferry, was a remote spot near Kingennie House and a few farms. By this time the line had reached 250 feet above sea level. Gagie Halt, opened by the LMS in the 1930s, was just over a mile further on. It served the nearby village of Wellbank and stood at about 350 feet. A sweeping curve through a cutting slewed the line in an easterly direction and the ascent continued above the headwaters of Pitairlie Burn to Monikie, seven and a half miles along the branch and 500 feet up. Another broad curve took the track in a northerly direction once more, and the summit at over 550 feet was reached at Skichen amid a scattering of farms. Kirkbuddo station (just over eleven miles from Broughty Ferry Junction) served a country house and more farms, with Fothringham Hill (820ft) forming a prominent feature to the

The Dundee - Forfar direct route emerged from a cutting to join the main line at Forfar North junction. On 18th December 1954 'Crab' 2-6-0 No 42800 negotiated the points with the residue of the daily pick up goods as Standard mogul No 76002 shunted the yard. Ahead lies Turin Hill, a hint of the attractive rolling countryside encountered by the railways to both Dundee and Arbroath.

On 8th January 1955 C16 4-4-2T No 67493 awaits departure from Barnhill (Angus) with the 12.41pm to Dundee East, a short working for the benefit of lunchtime commuters. The station building with its curious bay window can just be seen beyond the neat signal box, which was typical of the Forfar direct line. On the platform is a 1 in 67/1 in 200 gradient post, an indication of the undulating track ahead. Also visible is the small goods yard which dealt with more coal but less agricultural produce than those in the rural hinterland.

north west. A steady descent to 370 feet brought the line down to Kingsmuir station which served a roadside village just outside Forfar, and a little over two miles further on came the junction with the main line.

As with all routes across hilly country, earthworks were necessary on the Forfar direct line, and several long stretches were a succession of cuttings and embankments. Station buildings were small neat structures built of stone. Each had a steeply pitched roof at right angles to the track, and an unusual feature was the V shaped bay window, with its own pitched roof, set into the gable on the platform side. Passenger services were always fairly sparse, but the goods yards were hives of activity. Forfar to Dundee East passenger trains were withdrawn on 10th January 1955 resulting in the demise of all six intermediate stations. Kingsmuir - Forfar closed on 8th December 1958, the large flour mill at Monikie stopped providing traffic in the early 1960s and the pick-up goods ceased on 9th October 1967, all six yards then closing.

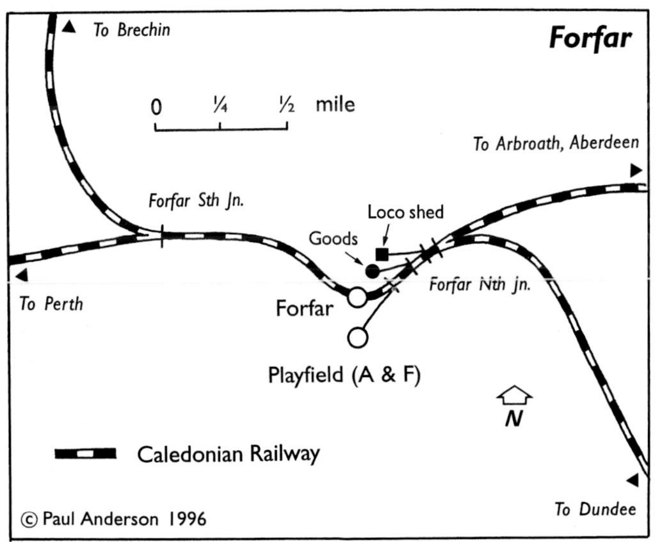

CARMYLLIE

From the late 1700s, many farmers around Greystone, Redford and Carmyllie dug small pits on their land and took stone roofing slates down to Arbroath and Dundee by cart. Some slabs found their way to Edinburgh, such was the demand. Eventually much larger quarries were opened up at Carmyllie to supply freestone for building tenements in the growing industrial towns further south. In the early 1850s they were owned by Fox Maule, Lord Panmure, the second Baron of Panmure, who decided to build a private mineral line down to Elliot, provided it only involved a 'moderate cost of construction'. Conveyance of agricultural produce was also anticipated. The Dundee & Arbroath regarded the branch as a potentially lucrative feeder and supplied old rails and chairs at bargain prices. In May 1854 horses began to haul wagons of stone from Carmyllie to Elliot over five miles of temporary track. Proper permanent way was completed in February 1855, enabling Dundee & Arbroath steam locomotives to venture into the Angus hills to collect building material for the far off tenements.

The Scottish North Eastern began working the line on 1st February 1864 and an Act of 1865 made it a statutory railway. By then no less than three hundred men were employed in the quarries, paving stones being the main product. A passenger service was suggested from time to time, but the expense of signalling and other improvements was deemed uneconomic. The Light Railway Act of 1896, requiring less stringent standards, provided the solution. On 6th August 1898 the branch was reconstituted as the Carmyllie Light Railway and passenger services began on 1st February 1900 - the first in Scotland to be operated under these new regulations. Mixed trains comprising both coaches and goods wagons were the norm, and only third class travel was on offer, tickets being issued by the guard. Services usually started from Arbroath, with time consuming shunts over the crossovers at Elliot Junction adding to the already pedestrian schedule. Passenger accommodation was limited (not that it mattered too much) for gradients as severe as 1 in 36 limited the length of trains.

Slow it might have been, but a journey up to Carmyllie was a pleasant trip for the casual traveller. From just above sea level at Elliot Junction the line climbed alongside Elliot Water past Kellie Glen and its castle. Arbilot village at 150 feet was served by a station a mile and a half from the junction. After just over two miles the branch reached Cuthlie Halt, 240 feet up and deriving its name from a nearby farm overlooking Elliot Water in a cleft. Progress diagonally up the valley slope revealed sweeping views of the hills to the west and led to Denhead, 370 feet high, three and a half miles from Elliot Junction and named after a farm next to the station. The ascent finished at Redford on the 500 feet contour. Lord Panmure's quarries were just ahead, but the tiny hamlet of Carmyllie lay over a mile away to the south west. As was to be expected, the stations were primitive affairs with basic timber buildings, but they only had to suffice for thirty years as the passenger service was withdrawn on 2nd December 1929. All four yards on the branch became unstaffed public sidings on 2nd May 1960 and finally succumbed on 24th May 1965 after stone traffic had long disappeared. A spur to the Metal Box factory at Elliot Junction was taken out of use on 29th July 1984 and the branch was no more. Elliot Junction itself closed to public goods traffic on 24th May 1965 and passenger facilities were withdrawn on 4th September 1967.

Above. **In teeming rain on 7th September 1963, inappropriately-named A2 Pacific No.60527 SUN CHARIOT sends smoke and steam into the trees as it sets off from Bridge of Dun with the 1.30pm Aberdeen - Glasgow Buchanan Street. A few wagons were scattered forlornly in the sidings, including a steel plate carrier and a Scottish Gas Board tar tanker.**

Below. **Class 5 4-6-0 No.44794 blows off impatiently as it waits for parcels traffic to be dealt with at Bridge of Dun on 18th May 1966. The neat Aberdeen Railway station house is on the left and a contemporary water tower to the right. There is also a glimpse of the fancy wooden footbridge and the very ornate canopy supports on the island platform.**

Chapter 3

MONTROSE AND BRECHIN

It could be argued that the triangle of country north east of Forfar and Arbroath does not belong in a book on Tayside. Indeed, the old market town of Brechin and the maritime settlement of Montrose look towards Aberdeen as much as Dundee. However, in railway terms this area neatly tied up the routes from the south, with the west coast Caledonian and east coast North British main lines meeting at legendary Kinnaber Junction. In fact nearly every mile of track in the Angus - Kincardineshire border district was associated to a greater or lesser extent with the drive to improve communications to and from the Grampian coast. In addition to two main lines, the network covered by this chapter included short links to the principal towns, a couple of rural routes in Strathmore, and a very attractive coastal branch.

The old Arbroath & Forfar provided a springing point for three of these projects. First came the Aberdeen Railway from Guthrie and Friockheim to Laurencekirk and the north, with branches to Brechin and Montrose. It was an important trunk route from the outset and eventually became the northern section of the Caledonian main line. North British access to Aberdeen was a less clear cut business and was not really effective until the Forth Bridge opened. At one stage the east coast passage looked like involving the Bervie branch, and even the vital Arbroath - Kinnaber Junction section functioned as a local line for several years. A possible short cut for Aberdeen - Euston expresses opened between Brechin and Forfar a century ago, but this link was destined to remain a pedestrian rural affair. About the same time, another bucolic branch wandered up to Edzell, and Brechin became something of a modest rail centre.

THE ABERDEEN RAILWAY

One of the most amazing proposals of the horse waggonway era was for a line from Crieff to Aberdeen via Strathmore, with branches to Arbroath and Montrose. Advocated by Robert Stevenson in the early 1820s, it remained a dream, but the idea of a national transport system never went away. During the mania years of 1844-45 Aberdeen became obsessed with railway promotion however, realising it would suffer economically by not being on the network. Strong-minded local businessmen planned lines to the north, west and south, and they wanted control over all the tracks within a hundred mile radius so that their destiny would not lie in the hands of companies based in Perth or Dundee.

There were two schools of thought for a route to the south; one favoured Strathmore, the other preferred the coast. Matters were resolved when the Aberdeen Railway was formed to build a line through Brechin to Forfar, and the Scottish Midland Junction Railway was launched to continue this southwards to Perth. All was love and light at first, but without telling its partner the Aberdeen Railway revised its alignment south of Laurencekirk and aimed for Guthrie and Friockheim on the Arbroath & Forfar line. The Scottish Midland Junction was deeply suspicious of the motives behind this change and Brechin was furious, as the town would now be bypassed. Nevertheless the new scheme was accepted by parliament and the Aberdeen Railway obtained its Act on 31st July 1845.

Construction work was concentrated on the easier southern section. Commencing around 160ft above sea level at Guthrie Junction, the line headed north eastwards and soon met the spur from Friockheim which had crossed Lunan Water on a small viaduct. By Glasterlaw station (two miles from Guthrie Junction) the track had climbed to about 200ft. A long cutting through Muirside of Kinnell led to a fairly sharp descent in the shadow of 433ft Wuddy Law. At Farnell Road (five miles) the rails were down to 60ft and low

J37 0-6-0 No.64602 climbing away from Bridge of Dun with the daily goods to Brechin on 18th May 1966. This delightful scene in late spring sunshine clearly shows the nature of the branch. Undulating country required a succession of earthworks; in this case an embankment crossing a dip in the fields of Balwyllo Farm.

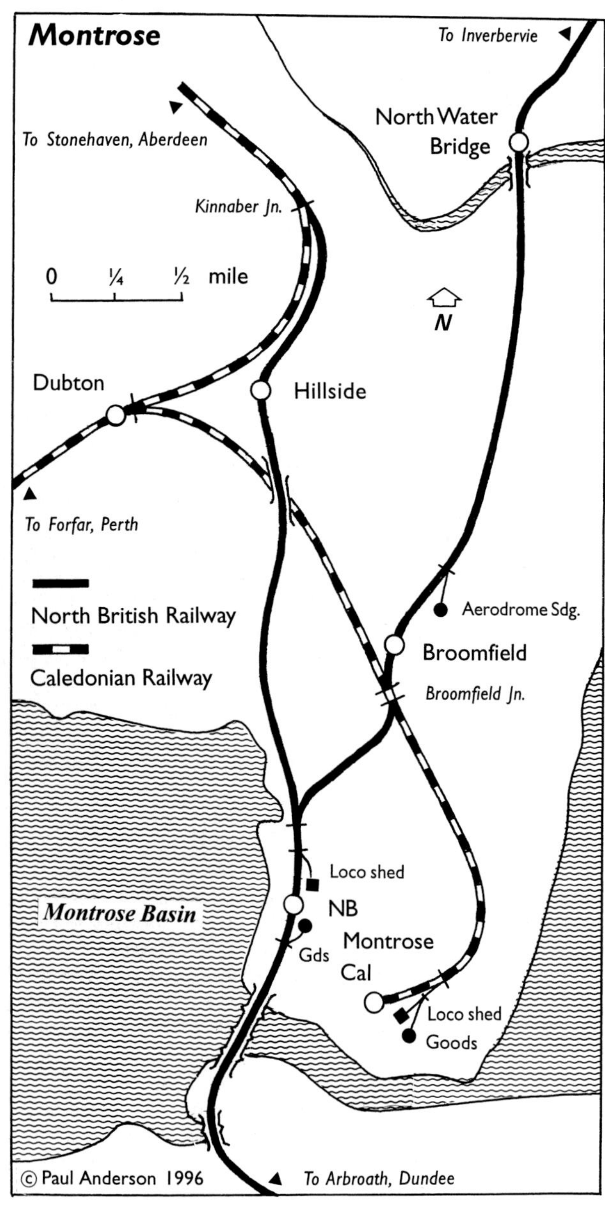

ground followed with Row Burn and Kinnaird Castle to the west. A span across the South Esk came before Bridge of Dun station (eight miles) just 10ft above sea level. Finally a gentle climb in a cutting brought the line to Dubton (just under 11 miles) and the 60ft contour again.

Bridge of Dun and Dubton were the junctions for branches to Brechin and Montrose respectively. Trade between these two towns was considerable and a waggonway link had been suggested as far back as 1819. Brechin, with a population of about 8,000 in 1848, was perched on a steep slope overlooking the South Esk and prospered as a market centre for eastern Strathmore. Its many red sandstone buildings included a squat little cathedral dating from around 1200 and remnants of a Celtic abbey completed two centuries earlier. Despite early hopes that it would be on a main line, the town had to accept a terminus at the end of a four mile branch from Bridge of Dun. This ventured along the northern slope of South Esk Valley and had a succession of cuttings and embankments to maintain a steady climb up to 130ft.

Montrose had around 16,000 inhabitants in the late 1840s. Spacious and dignified, it stood on a broad tongue of land seawards of a tidal lagoon where the South Esk swelled out before flowing through a picturesque estuary leading to Montrose Bay. The harbour was on the north side of this channel and faced an attractive shoreline rising from Inchbraoch to the low cliffs of Scurdie Ness. From 60ft at Dubton the three mile branch descended gently, first curving southwards around undulating ground at Mains of Hedderwick, then heading straight for the sandy Links of Montrose. A sharp turn to the west brought the line close to the town centre and a few hundred yards from the quayside, which was served by a branch from the goods yard.

During celebrations on 27th January 1848, the Aberdeen Railway directors were taken by special train from Montrose to Brechin and Guthrie. Five days later, on 1st February, the Dubton - Guthrie/ Friockheim section, together with the Montrose and Brechin branches, were opened for public traffic and the Arbroath & Forfar was leased. Although the company was able to serve five important towns, including Dundee, the rest of the main line languished in an unfinished state and some construction sites were deserted. By summer 1848 the company was in deep financial trouble and elements in Aberdeen had actually become hostile to the railway. But the shareholders rallied, further capital was raised and the trunk route was completed in stages, passenger trains from the outskirts of Aberdeen commencing on 1st February 1850. The section north of Dubton began with a sweeping curve round Hillside, a one and a half mile cutting at Logie and a viaduct across the North Esk at Marykirk (fifteen and a half miles from Guthrie Junction). A steady climb through a three mile cutting took the line up to 250ft at Laurencekirk (nineteen and a half miles) overlooked by the long ridge of 900ft Hill of Garvock.

The impact of the line was immediate and dramatic. Journey times for mail and passengers were cut overnight, Aberdeen's manufacturing industry was given a boost, local granite found new markets and regular cattle and fish trains ran to London. Despite its financial difficulties the company provided the area with some delightful station buildings, all of them in local sandstone. Tudor cottages with steep gables, tall chimneys and a very dignified bay window facing the platform were put up at Bridge of Dun and Dubton. The slightly later station at Laurencekirk was a beautiful creation with matching buildings featuring stepped gables, tiny canopies and no less than four dignified bay windows. Brechin gained a square two-storey structure with a low hipped roof, reminiscent of a large town house. At Montrose, the directors' special on the opening day had to use a temporary station in Rotten Row, but the permanent structure, completed in 1849, was a larger version of the Tudor cottages and featured a short overall roof sheltering the platform road and an adjacent siding. Here the bay windows were elevated to form dormers in the roof.

From 12th February 1851 to 31st July 1854 the Aberdeen Railway and Arbroath & Forfar were worked by the Scottish Central. No doubt this confirmed the earlier fears of the Scottish Midland Junction, but that company merged with the Aberdeen Railway to form the Scottish North Eastern on 29th July 1856. With the expansionist policies pursued by both the Caledonian and North British over the following decade, the Perth - Aberdeen line became a desirable acquisition, and on 10th August 1866 the Scottish North Eastern was absorbed by the former. But parliament was concerned about one major company having a monopoly of Aberdeen traffic and granted the North British running powers over the whole of the acquired system. These were not exercised with any vigour at first, although through carriages from Burntisland to Aberdeen via Dundee, Arbroath, Friockheim and Bridge of Dun were operated following the opening of the first Tay Bridge in 1878. From 1883 North British trains headed north over the Arbroath - Kinnaber Junction line (see later) and when the second Tay Bridge and Forth Bridge opened a few years later, the scene was set for a real east coast challenge.

A fine panorama of the fishing harbour of Gourdon, typifying the grand coastal scenery on the northern part of the Bervie branch. With Doolie Ness and Horse Crook Bay as a backdrop, English Electric type 1 No.D8028 leaves Gourdon with the Easter weekend 'Scottish Rambler' on 22nd April 1962. It is difficult to envisage this stretch of track as part of the East Coast main line!

Competition for London - Aberdeen traffic reached theatrical proportions with the famous races to the Grampian coast during 1895. LNWR and Caledonian engines tore along the west coast line from Euston via Crewe, Carlisle and Perth, whilst Great Northern, North Eastern and North British locos pounded along east coast tracks from King's Cross via Newcastle, Edinburgh and Dundee. The routes met at Kinnaber Junction, a seemingly insignificant place named after a farm some distance away, but the first train there was the winner and the signal box became the focus of national attention for a few hectic weeks.

After this reckless game the former Aberdeen Railway settled down to a less frantic pace, carrying copious amounts of goods and passenger traffic in a steady yet efficient manner. Montrose and Brechin were not neglected. Southbound expresses stopped at Dubton and northbound trains paused at Bridge of Dun, providing connections with the two towns. Local services followed the fast services in each direction. Over the years the line to Aberdeen has seen motive power in all shapes and sizes, from early single wheelers to the massive P2 2-8-2 built by the LNER. Recently there has been much pressure for electrification, but this only involves the section north of erstwhile Kinnaber Junction, for the east coast route has outlived the lines opened in 1848.

After the spectacular coastal approach, Inverbervie terminus was a bit of an anti-climax. The short platform and little timber building were typical of Montrose & Bervie Railway architecture and seemed almost apologetic against the robust sandstone houses in the background. With a sprinkling of snow on the track, J37 0-6-0 No.64602 was about to depart with the 3.15pm return goods trip to Montrose on 28th December 1964. The short train included two vans of boxed fish.

The first closure came remarkably early, Glasterlaw losing its passenger service between December 1857 and April 1881. Caledonian passenger trains between Dundee and Aberdeen finished on 1st February 1908, rendering the Friockheim - Glasterlaw spur redundant. It was lifted in 1917 for the war effort. Dubton - Montrose locals were diverted into the former North British station from 30th April 1934 and the terminus was closed to passengers. The service itself was withdrawn on 4th August 1952, along with that to Brechin, Dubton station closing at the same time. Stopping trains along the main line ceased on 11th June 1956, resulting in the closure of Farnell Road, Craigo and Marykirk stations. Glasterlaw had already gone, on 2nd April 1951. The goods yard at Dubton finished on 15th June 1964, followed by those at Farnell Road and Bridge of Dun on 25th January 1965. The line from Broomfield to Dubton closed on 20th June 1963 and goods facilities at Montrose East and the harbour were withdrawn on 19th June

Seen from Rossie Island in scorching weather, V2 2-6-2 No.60838 rumbles across Montrose Viaduct with a northbound summer Saturday relief on 4th July 1959. This sturdy looking structure replaced Thomas Bouch's feeble effort before the line opened. Beyond the piers is a concrete bridge carrying the main road from Arbroath. It opened in 1928 and was a fair copy of the 1828 suspension bridge which preceded it.

1967. With the end of Glasgow - Aberdeen expresses via Strathmore on 4th September 1967, Bridge of Dun and Laurencekirk stations were erased from the map. This just left the Kinnaber Junction - Brechin goods branch which survived until 1981, as detailed later.

EAST COAST GENESIS

For the past three decades all trains from Glasgow and Edinburgh to Aberdeen have used the line through Dundee, Arbroath and Montrose. Although the east coast route ultimately triumphed over that through Strathmore, establishing it was a convoluted business involving Great North of Scotland Railway disenchantment in Aberdeen, a local branch which became a pawn in big railway politics, and sheer North British determination. Indeed, the section between Arbroath and Kinnaber Junction was a relative latecomer in the Victorian era of railway construction. The saga ended in 1890; it had taken nearly a quarter of a century to resolve, though the roots actually lay back in the late 1850s.

Shortly after the Scottish North Eastern was formed in 1856, a local company called the Montrose & Bervie Railway promoted a line along the rocky Kincardineshire shoreline to Inverbervie. This had long been known as the 'smugglers coast' and included many secluded and mysterious places such as Big Rob's Cove, Horse Crook Bay and Ararat. Inverbervie itself, a small fishing settlement at the mouth of Bervie Water, was made a Royal Burgh in 1342 shortly after King David II landed there, ending a nine year exile in France. The village was credited with the invention of linen spinning machinery in 1787. On 3rd July 1860 the thirteen mile Montrose & Bervie received its Act, but could not raise the necessary cash and tried to get the Scottish North Eastern to build its line, to no avail.

The focus of attention then turned to Aberdeen where the Great North of Scotland Railway was in dispute with the Scottish North Eastern over junction arrangements and Buchan traders wanted a more efficient route south. As a result, the Scottish Northern Junction was formed, in 1861, to build a main line from Kintore, north west of Aberdeen, to Stonehaven some way south of the city. The GN of S simultaneously acquired a substantial interest in the Montrose & Bervie, on the understanding that the local concern would extend its proposed route ten miles north to Stonehaven and fourteen miles south to the independent Dundee & Arbroath. Retaliation from southern interests came with plans for a line from Arbroath to Stonehaven via Inverbervie. Neither scheme materialised and the Dundee & Arbroath was taken over by the Scottish North Eastern. The GN of S lost interest in an independent route south and sold its holdings in the Montrose & Bervie, so the local line was left to its own devices.

Nevertheless the branch was built, opening throughout on 1st November 1865 and worked by Scottish North Eastern locos. It was a very scenic stretch of railway, beginning at Broomfield Junction north of Montrose and striding across the North Esk near Kinnaber by means of a high stone viaduct. After a cliff top section to St. Cyrus, the line wandered inland for a while before descending to the rocky shore at Johnshaven. The track then curved round the back of Gourdon village and continued along the coast to a terminus close to Bervie Bay. Architecturally, the stations were undistinguished, all seven of them having basic single storey buildings with horizontal timber planking and brick chimneys. The Montrose & Bervie was very much an impoverished local line; staff did not have uniforms at first and two stationmasters were dismissed for helping themselves to cash! When the Caledonian took over the Scottish North Eastern in August 1866, charges for the use of Montrose terminus became excessive, so the Bervie company opened a station at Broomfield. Rates were reduced from February 1867 and the former arrangements resumed, but Broomfield remained open until 31st December 1878.

As noted earlier, the 1866 Act sanctioned North British running powers over the Caledonian to Aberdeen. It also stipulated that the Dundee & Arbroath would become joint property if, as anticipated, a line was built along the coast to Montrose. Matters came to a head with the Tay Bridge Act of 1871, and shortly afterwards the North British, Arbroath & Montrose Railway received parliamentary approval. This was a most peculiar concern. On the one hand it was an intensely parochial affair, with many local councillors and other worthies on the committee seeing the railway as a godsend to fishing and farming communities. Conversely it was to be built to main line standards as a 'necessary complement to the Tay Bridge' and heralded in Montrose as a

***Top.* That glorious summer again. V2 2-6-2 No.60873 COLDSTREAMER awaits the right of way at Montrose with the 3.10pm Aberdeen - Edinburgh Waverley on 4th July 1959. The three Gresley teak-bodied coaches at the front of the train looked particularly fine. Conflats were prominent in the yard, whilst the passenger station with its modern concrete lamp standards (contrasting with the 1881 buildings) can be seen on the left.**

***Above.* Brechin station presented a very appealing facade to the town, as can be seen in this 22nd April 1962 view. Its distinctive appearance stemmed from the semi-circular clock housing complete with ball finial, and the full width canopy. Presumably the delicate wrought ironwork once announced 'Caledonian Railway', Most of this work dated from the 1895 enlargement, but the 1848 station house can be seen on the left.**

trunk route. Construction presented no problems but progress was painfully slow and the line was still far from complete when the Tay Bridge collapsed.

Although its main purpose had disappeared overnight, the Arbroath & Montrose opened from St. Vigean's Junction to Inverkeilor on 1st October 1880 and on to Lunan Bay seven days later. Then came the saga of the viaduct across Montrose Basin, Thomas Bouch's last bridge. The engineer had been commissioned to build the line partly because of his experience with the Tay Bridge, but after the latter failed, his spans across the South Esk at Montrose underwent rigorous tests with stationary and moving trains. In little more than a day it was twisted and distorted throughout. Demolition and reconstruction proceeded quickly and the section from Lunan Bay to Kinnaber Junction opened on 1st March 1881, a local passenger service from Arbroath to Montrose beginning at the same time. Through trains between Dundee and Aberdeen started on 1st May 1883.

St. Vigean's Junction - Kinnaber Junction was nearly sixteen miles and the line began with a gentle climb out of the Brothock Valley north of Arbroath. The rails then curved north eastwards to Letham Grange station (two miles) and reached 110 feet above sea level at Cauldcots (almost four miles). A slight drop through the village of Inverkeilor (just over five miles) led to a curved viaduct over Lunan Water. After negotiating a steep and indented hillside, the line passed through Lunan Bay station (nearly eight miles) and climbed to 165 feet to get behind the cliffs at Black Jack and Bloddin Harbour. The descent to Montrose was by means of a series of long curves, mainly in cuttings. A short viaduct took the railway on to Rossie Island and this was followed by the much more lengthy structure over the South Esk estuary. After Montrose station (thirteen miles) more curves led to Hillside (almost fifteen miles) and Kinnaber Junction. At first only one track was laid, but the formation and bridges - with the exception of Montrose Viaduct - were designed for double track. Stations were Spartan brick and timber affairs, although a substantial structure was erected at Montrose.

A one and a half mile spur was put in from Broomfield Junction to the main line at Montrose so that Bervie trains could use the new station, and the local company was absorbed by the North British on 1st October 1881. This did not stop the branch becoming involved in railway politics yet again. In retaliation for North British incursions into its territory elsewhere, the Caledonian exercised its right to run trains to Bervie, so from 2nd August 1897 to 30th September 1898 the coastal villages had separate passenger services to each Montrose station. With this dispute out of the way and the Aberdeen races over, the Arbroath - Kinnaber Junction lines settled down as an integral part of the East Coast main line.

Hillside closed to passengers in February 1927, followed by the other local stations on 22nd September 1930, leaving just Montrose. In 1928 meanwhile, the line (except for Montrose Viaduct) had been doubled. From 1934 LMS trains between Dubton and Montrose were diverted over the Broomfield spur into the LNER station. There was a bit of excitement early in World War 2 when a low flying aircraft demolished the upper part of Broomfield Junction signal box. Passenger trains to Inverbervie (the station had been renamed in July 1926) were withdrawn on 1st October 1951. Goods facilities at local stations on the main line were withdrawn gradually - Letham Grange 1st July 1959; Lunan Bay 18th May 1964; Hillside 21st June 1965; Cauldcots 16th August 1965. The Bervie branch lost its daily goods train on 23rd May 1966. Two passenger trips, organised locally, took place on Sunday 22nd, and were hauled by J37 No.64547. Kinnaber Junction box was abolished on 25th July 1982, having been kept open merely for private siding traffic at Hillside - a real come-down from its heady days back in 1895. Inverkeilor goods closed in April 1983 and Montrose coal yard finished the following August. To end on a positive note, Montrose gained a fine new station building in 1984.

Top. **The daily goods shunting at Careston on a grey 25th February 1961. This view, looking west towards Forfar, shows the ample station building well. It was typical of those provided by the Forfar & Brechin Railway.**

Above. **On the cold damp morning of 25th February 1961, veteran Caledonian 'Jumbo' 0-6-0 No.57345 shunts Justinhaugh yard, steam leaking from every joint. Bare trees peering through the mist and an overgrown platform with a sagging timber building added to the forlorn atmosphere - but this could have been part of the West Coast main line.**

BRECHIN BRANCHES

The former Aberdeen Railway branch from Bridge of Dun was the only line into Brechin for nearly half a century, plenty of passengers and goods traffic originating in this prosperous town. This was also the railhead for eastern Strathmore and the nearby Grampian foothills where horses and carts were the only way of moving produce. During the last decade of the nineteenth century, attempts were made to link this rural hinterland with the national network, resulting in new branches to Forfar and Edzell. Brechin station was enlarged at the same time. They were attractive lines, ambling across rich farmland on fertile soil and affording delightful views of the distant Braes of Angus. Although quite well used by passengers for a while, the two branches were vulnerable to mechanised road transport and the district did not develop - in fact the population actually declined. Goods traffic was more important and continued well after passenger services ceased - this applied to the original Brechin branch as well.

When the Aberdeen Railway made its controversial decision to head for Guthrie rather than Brechin and Forfar, it left the eastern end of Strathmore somewhat isolated, besides adding eight miles to the overall journey from Perth. The Forfar & Brechin Railway aimed to fill the gap and was supported by the Caledonian, which agreed to work the line and guaranteed a 3.5% dividend. A suggestion from the local company, however, that its tracks could be modified to take main line trains, was immediately rejected on the grounds that this would mean bypassing Forfar, and would also subject expresses to steep climbs in both directions. So the Forfar & Brechin was destined to remain a rural backwater.

Services between Forfar and Brechin began on 7th January 1895 for goods and 1st June 1895 for passengers. From Forfar South Junction, actually north west of the town, the fourteen and a half mile branch swung northwards past Quilkoe and Carse Hill, a succession of cuttings and embankments crossing the headwaters of Lemno Burn. Having reached nearly 300ft at Wolflaw, a climb of 100ft from Forfar, the line turned eastwards to Justinhaugh station (four miles) overlooking the South Esk and dominated by the 750ft Hill of Finavon to the South. After crossing the river the railway reached Tannadice station (just over five miles). Another bridge across the wooded valley of Noran Water marked the half way point. After a stretch hemmed in by hillslopes on both sides, the branch reached open country at Careston (just over nine miles). In the distance the Cairngorm foothills soon rose to well over 2,000ft and wild slopes with enigmatic names like Potty Leadnar and Manywee displayed a very different landscape. A cutting through the 350ft ridge at Broomfield marked the summit and a sharp descent took the line down to 160ft at Brechin, sweeping round the northern edge of the town to lose the last hundred feet or so. A spur to the Bridge of Dun line avoiding the terminus was also provided.

Stations on the Forfar & Brechin were quite generous considering the nature of the branch. They had wide and fairly long side platforms with substantial timber buildings featuring low pitched roofs, a modicum of decoration, little finials and a full length canopy. They proved more than adequate for the traffic on offer; Tannadice had a population of about 1,300 when the line opened - a quarter of a century later it was down to just over 900. Careston's scattered farms could only offer about 200 potential customers. Three or four trains each way sufficed.

Edzell is a neatly planned estate village on the North Esk where fertile Strathmore gives way to the bleak Grampian heights. Along with nearby Fettercairn in the Howe of the Mearns, it became a focus for upland farms such as those in straggling Glen Esk, and boasted a fine castle - noted for its walled sculpture garden. The title of the branch line which ventured here actually summed up the role of the village, but nevertheless sounded like some sort of comprehensive suburban system. Opened on 1st June 1896, the Brechin & Edzell District Railway managed to remain nominally independent until absorbed by the LMS in 1923. Its five and a quarter miles of switchback track left the Forfar line on the north side of Brechin and immediately climbed from 250ft to nearly 300ft in half a mile. A steady descent took the line down to 190ft at a bridge over Cruick Water. Stracathro station (three miles) was named after a large house just under two miles away, although it was called Inchbare until 1st October 1912, then Dunlappie until 1st November 1912. Just beyond here the branch was at a lowly 145ft where it crossed the North Esk. More embankments and cuttings, characteristic features of its weaving course northwards, led the line to Edzell back around the 200ft contour.

The great and the good at Forfar South Junction on 14th October 1961. V2 2-6-2 No.60919 storms towards the racing ground of Strathmore with the 11.30am Aberdeen - Glasgow Buchanan Street express as ex-Caledonian 4-4-0 No.54500 waits impatiently with cattle wagons from Careston, on the truncated Brechin branch

The terminus consisted of a single platform with a short bay for vans. Alongside it was a spacious goods yard with sidings fanning out to a timber transit shed, a loading bank served by a crane, and a modest coal depot. Besides its regular residential and business traffic, the branch carried numerous tourists during the spring and summer, attracted by the Grampian foothills. A reasonable timetable reflected this; in 1928 for example there were seven departures from Brechin on weekdays, with a couple of extras on Saturdays. As on the other Brechin branches, Caledonian 0-4-4Ts with two coach sets were used, some trains conveying goods wagons as well.

Brechin station was substantially improved to cater for the increased traffic. An extra side platform with a bay was provided and ample canopies added, but the most attractive feature was a new entrance building, with an iron and glass veranda and a prominent clock. The goods depot was enlarged, a long single road engine shed was built, and a large signal box erected.

Closure of the Brechin branches was a prolonged process. The short-lived avoiding line went first, lifted in 1917 to help the war effort. Passenger trains to Edzell were withdrawn on 27th April 1931, although they were reinstated experimentally between 4th July and 27th September 1938. Services from Brechin to Forfar and Bridge of Dun ceased on 4th August 1952, a rather early date for a town of this importance to lose its station. Brechin to Careston was abandoned on 17th March 1958, thus severing the through route. Stracathro goods closed on 7th December 1959 and Tannadice yard finished on 3rd October 1960. Freight facilities at Edzell and Careston were withdrawn on 7th September 1964 but the Forfar - Justinhaugh section lasted until 4th September 1967.

Finally, the original Brechin branch closed officially on 4th May 1981, the last goods working being on 30th April when all wagons were removed. Large crowds watched a diesel multiple unit special on 2nd May, to the accompaniment of exploding detonators. Fortunately this was not the end. The Brechin Railway Preservation Society had been formed in 1979 to purchase the line to Bridge of Dun and moved into the dilapidated terminus during 1980. Since then it has gone from strength to strength and now provides a taste of steam days in the Tayside area.

Departures from Brechin, Monday to Saturday, summer 1948

7.00am	Forfar (via Careston)
8.30am	Montrose (via Dubton)
9.33am	Bridge of Dun
10.25am	Montrose (via Dubton)
12.30pm	Montrose (via Dubton)
1.58pm	Montrose (via Dubton)
2.02pm	Forfar (via Careston)
4.21pm	Montrose (via Dubton)
5.10pm	Bridge of Dun
6.08pm	Montrose (via Dubton)
6.15pm	Forfar (via Careston)
7.38pm	Montrose (via Dubton)
10.10pm	SO Montrose (via Dubton)

SO Sats only.

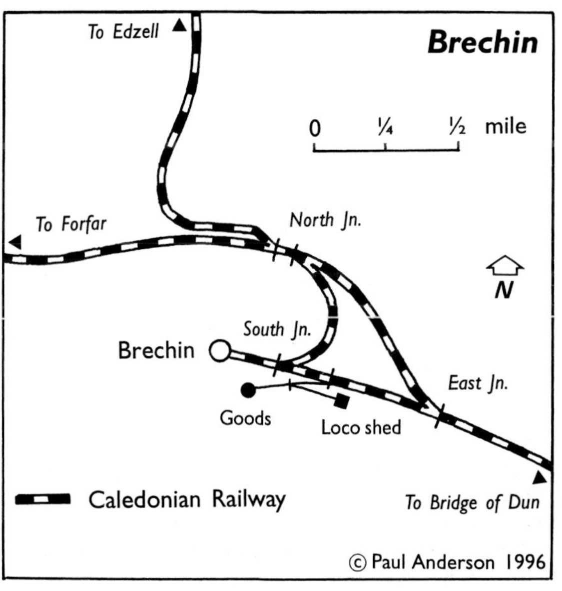

Above. Coupar Angus station on 29th August 1966. The island platform has a typical late-19th century Caledonian building with a big apron canopy, although this one was less decorative than some examples - on the Cathcart Circle in Glasgow, for instance. Construction of the Scottish Midland Junction obliterated all traces of the primitive Newtyle & Coupar Angus Railway. The town centre is on the left and goods sidings curve away to the right.

Below. A2 Pacific No.60531 BAHRAM pulls out of Forfar and heads for the fast Strathmore section with the 1.30pm Aberdeen-Glasgow Buchanan Street, on 14th October 1961.

Chapter 4

STRATHMORE

When considering the history of the Caledonian main line south of Forfar, it is necessary to go back to the very early days of railways again, for the route through western Strathmore was partially based on two somewhat eccentric feeder branches of the Dundee & Newtyle. Strathmore literally means 'big valley', but it is not a valley in the strict sense. Rather, it is a broad and beautiful lowland stretching for over forty miles from the Tay valley north of Perth to the North Sea coast at Montrose. In the area under consideration, Strathmore is bordered by the Grampian mountains to the north and the Sidlaw Hills to the south. Although the River Isla is the main watercourse, there are numerous minor tributaries, creating a series of gentle dips and low rises on the valley floor. This is extremely fertile country with prosperous farms and fields of Aberdeen Angus cattle providing the best beef in the world. There are also several large country houses and castles, with Glamis the most famous and romantic of them all. Industry, in the form of jute manufacturing was present as well, largely concentrated in the attractive towns and villages towards the northern edge.

The Dundee & Newtyle merely peeped at Strathmore, but soon put out tentacles which explored and exploited the rich lowland as far as Coupar Angus and Glamis. After just over a decade these primitive branches became part of the trunk route from London to Aberdeen. In the mania years this was almost inevitable, for Strathmore was a natural routeway between the 'Granite City', Buchan and Inverness to the north and Perth, Glasgow and Carlisle to the south. The railway along the western part of the valley got off to a fairly pedestrian start, but with negligible gradients and few curves it eventually became one of the fastest main lines in Britain. Branches were built to the little towns of Blairgowrie, Alyth and Kirriemuir, whilst a much improved route to Dundee was established once the Newtyle line inclines were bypassed.

Ex-Caledonian 0-4-4T No.55200, with paint burnt off what appears to be a genuine Caley smokebox door, takes water at Forfar shed on 18th December 1954. For decades, these sturdy little engines hauled most passenger trains on the Blairgowrie, Alyth, Kirriemuir and Brechin branches, as well as the services to Dundee from Alyth Junction and Forfar.

GLAMIS CASTLE

NEWTYLE AND THE MAIN LINE

Details of the Dundee & Newtyle Railway can be found in Chapter 1, although the northern extremity was deliberately left vague as it properly belongs to Strathmore. From Auchterhouse, the long summit section pursued on almost level course across a broad plain where the Sidlaw slopes drew back. But at Pitnappie, 532 feet above sea level, the topography changed abruptly. A fearsome ridge of volcanic rock forming the landward edge of the hill range stood in the way, although it parted between Hatton Hill and Newtyle Hill (both over 860 feet) to give a narrow pass known as the Glack of Newtyle. The railway squeezed through this crack, descending at 1 in 13 for 1,025 yards to end at 288 feet on the edge of Strathmore. Hatton Incline was single track and operated by a 20hp condensing engine working at 4.5lb per square inch steam pressure. At the

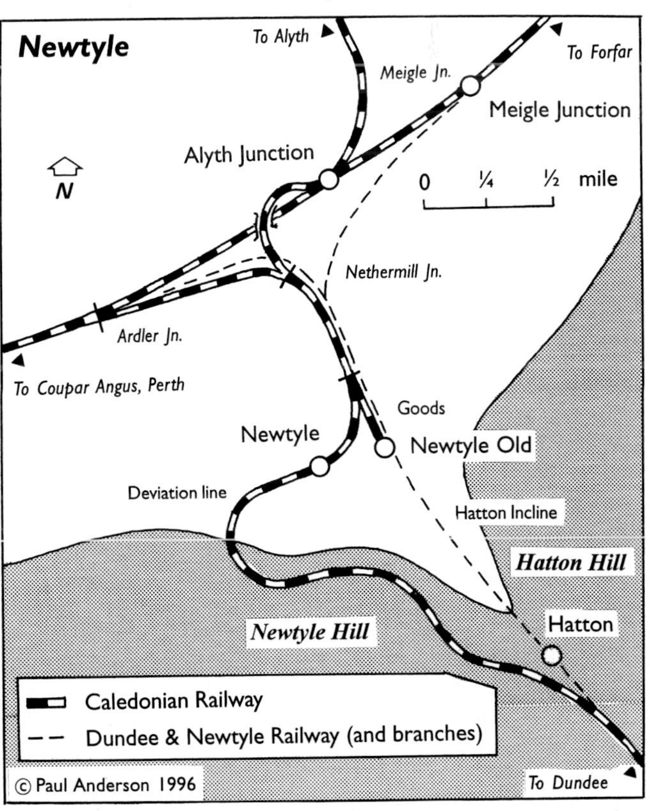

Blairgowrie terminus on the last day, Saturday 8th January 1955. The train is the 2.55pm to Dundee West via Newtyle, headed by Tay Bridge B1 4-6-0 No.61101. Although the modest overall roof and goods shed were conventional enough and must have looked quite attractive in their heyday, the residual platform canopy presented a most odd appearance.

bottom was Newtyle station, a plain yet pleasant little brick and stone building with a full length canopy, no less than four chimneys, and a short platform. To reach it, trains had to pass *through* an adjoining stone goods shed which covered two tracks. Passenger services from Dundee began on 3rd April 1832.

Two small companies were soon formed to extend the Dundee line into Strathmore. The Newtyle & Coupar Angus Railway received its Act on 21st July 1835 and the Newtyle & Glammiss Railway was authorised nine days later. Coupar Angus was a small but important market town on a low ridge above the River Isla and grew up close to a wealthy Cistercian abbey, founded in 1164 but destroyed in 1559. Glammiss (now spelt Glamis) was a neat farming village on the edge of the Sidlaw Hills. It has long been famous for its magnificent castle, a large medieval tower house which was transformed into a baronial palace with clusters of turrets during the late 17th century. The Coupar Angus line was just over five miles long and opened in February 1837 with an intermediate station at Ardler. The Glamis branch extended for 7.5 miles and included a station at Eassie as well as a couple of roadside depots for loading agricultural produce. It also opened during 1837 and four passenger trains a week began on 4th June 1838. Both railways were 4ft 6.5in gauge and combined at Nether Mill of Newtyle for the short 1 in 100 climb to an end on junction with the Dundee line.

The branches were operated by horse traction, although a Dundee & Newtyle engine worked to Coupar Angus at busy times and ventured to Glamis occasionally. Passenger trains, normally consisting of just one or two coaches, averaged less than 8 mph. However, it seems that from 1837 to 1841 speed on the Coupar Angus line increased dramatically when there was a gale blowing. In such conditions two poles were fitted to a passenger carriage and a tarpaulin sheet slung between them. With the help of this sail, the vehicle could reach 20 mph, its usual motive power trotting happily along behind in case the train was becalmed! The two lines were a byword for economy. One Newtyle & Glammiss report suggested that open trucks used for grain, flax and potatoes would make 'excellent summer coaches'.

With the explosion of railway promotion in 1844-45, Strathmore became a focus of attention, and with it the primitive branches. The Scottish Midland Junction Railway received its Act on 31st July 1845 and was authorised to incorporate the Newtyle & Coupar Angus and Newtyle & Glammiss in its 32.5 mile line from Perth to Forfar. Purchase of the local lines was completed in January 1846. Glamis to Eassie was closed for reconstruction in July 1846, Eassie to Newtyle followed in October 1847 and the Coupar Angus line finished in November 1847. Scottish Midland Junction passenger services between Perth and Forfar commenced on 20th August 1848 after an extravagant opening day which involved bands, processions, a banquet and speeches with toasts well into the early hours. The Meigle Junction-Newtyle section reopened at the same time for Dundee traffic and the first London-Aberdeen train passed through Strathmore on 1st April 1850.

The Perth-Coupar Angus section involved a fair amount of earthworks and other civil engineering work (see Chapter 6) but east of here it was relatively easy going. Once the 200 feet contour was reached, the line more or less kept to this level as far as Forfar. The old branches were laid directly on the ground surface for the most part, but some modest cuttings and embankments were required for the new formation east of Glamis. To the south, the steep edge of the Sidlaw Hills was a constant companion, a mile or so away from the railway, while there were fine views of the distant Grampians from the opposite carriage window.

On 29th July 1856 the Scottish Midland Junction merged with the Aberdeen Railway to form the Scottish North Eastern, and this in turn became part of the Caledonian system on 10th August 1866. Although the Caley had inherited a trunk route, it was not a particularly fast stretch of line. Scottish Midland Junction bridges were of wooden construction and despite the fact that they had been superbly built by craftsmen, time was beginning to take its toll. The constant passage of trains caused stresses and water seeped between the laminated timber and began to rot it. Sections had to be replaced at frequent intervals, but in many instances the whole structure was weak and speed restrictions were imposed. Safety matters came to the forefront in the wake of the Tay Bridge disaster, so a replacement programme was put into operation. By 1888 all the Strathmore bridges consisted of iron and stone, speeds had increased markedly, and the scene was set for the races to Aberdeen.

BLAIRGOWRIE, ALYTH AND KIRRIEMUIR

Within thirteen years of the Perth-Forfar route opening, three branches had struck northwards across Strathmore to small towns in the shadow of the Grampian foothills. For over a century these little railways conveyed agricultural produce and, for most of that period, their passenger services provided links with the rest of Tayside. But the lines to Blairgowrie, Alyth and Kirriemuir did not prevent a decline in population at their respective termini - industrial towns in the central belt mushroomed at the expense of rural areas, especially market centres with old fashioned industry. Ironically, the trend has reversed since the railways closed.

By any standards, Blairgowrie enjoys a lovely setting. Together with neighbouring Rattray, it tumbles down the steep slopes of the River Ericht valley on the very edge of the Grampians. Immediately north, beautiful Glenshee leads into the mountains, overlooked by the 1,400 feet summits of Knock of Balmyle and Drumderg. To the south, Strathmore stretches away towards the River Isla. The four mile Coupar Angus-Blairgowrie branch was an early Scottish Midland Junction project, opening for passengers on 1st August 1855 and goods on 21st

August. It was built to serve what was an important jute manufacturing town with more than 6,000 inhabitants, double the population of 1800. This was also an important area for growing soft fruit, notably raspberries. From its junction at Coupar Angus, on the 200 feet contour, the line curved sharply to the north, then cut through a ridge before crossing the River Isla at about 130 feet. From here it was uphill again to 200 feet and the track stayed at this level, paralleling the old military road. Beyond Rosemount (2.75 miles) the branch curved slightly north westwards as it approached Blairgowrie and ran parallel to the River Ericht for a while. An overall timber roof sheltered the inner end of the single platform terminus close to Blairgowrie town centre.

The branch required very little in the way of earthworks, but the Isla bridge was a substantial undertaking. It consisted of twelve timber spans and extended for almost 400 feet. In bad winters it received a severe battering from ice blocks carried by the swollen river as cold black water surged down from the Grampians. February 1881 was a particularly desperate time and on the night of the 3rd the engineer leading a team fighting to save the structure reported, 'standing on the viaduct was very much like being on the deck of a swift river steamer; there was the same tremulous motion and the recurring strokes of the ice among the piles made a very good imitation of the paddle floats'. It was replaced by girders and masonry shortly afterwards.

Alyth, five miles from Blairgowrie, is a busy little town overshadowed by Hill of Alyth and Hill of Loyal. It straddles Alyth Burn which cascades down from the slopes of Balduff Hill to join the River Isla somewhat to the east. As at Blairgowrie, there was jute manufacturing, but this was a smaller place, having a population of less than 3,500 in the mid 1800s. Its 5.5 mile branch from the main Coupar Angus-Forfar route was built by the independent Alyth Railway, opening for traffic on 2nd September 1861. The line began at a new junction station, initially called Meigle, then curved across a minor valley on an embankment. After cutting through a low ridge near Belmont Castle, the branch reached Meigle (a mile and a half) where the village station was called Fullarton at first, just to add to the confusion. The single track continued across the grain of the land, slicing through another ridge, then spanning Dean Water and the River Isla in quick succession.

This was the lowest point on the branch at 135 feet and from here there was a gentle rise to Mucketlands, then a steady climb to 300 feet in just over a mile. On the way was Jordanstone station (3.5 miles) and the curiously named farms of Silvie and Selvie. The line emerged from a cutting just beyond the summit revealing a fine view of the Alyth Burn valley with 968 feet Hill of Alyth as a backdrop. Alyth station was a pleasant little terminus on the edge of the town. It featured a fair-sized building and parallel timber train sheds with pitched roofs, one over the single platform and its track, the other sheltering the goods dock. The Alyth Railway was transferred to the Caledonian in 1875.

Kirriemuir is nine miles east of Alyth and half that distance from Forfar. Rather than snuggling up to the mountains, the red sandstone town stands on relatively level ground well into Strathmore, the Grampian ramparts of Culhawk Hill and Means Hill rearing up some two miles to the north. Kirriemuir's most famous son was undoubtedly Sir James Barrie, creator of Peter Pan. He was born in 1860 when the railway link to Forfar was being built. For some obscure reason, the supposed town ball also featured in one of the bawdiest rugby songs! The modest three mile branch from the main line was opened on 12th August 1861, around the same time as the Alyth Railway, but this time it was a Scottish North Eastern project. From around 200 feet at Kirriemuir Junction station the single track curved gently north westwards on a low embankment before climbing steadily past Mains of Ballindarg to Balmuckety, nearly 300 feet up. This was followed by tortuous curves through an

Former Caley 'Jumbo' 0-6-0 No.57441 rounding a special at Kirriemuir on 16th June 1960. The pleasant passenger station with its generous red sandstone building had closed almost eight years previously, although it still looked in remarkably serviceable condition. The goods yard on the right, and thus the branch, survived for another five years.

Kirriemuir Junction station was a remarkable survivor, no doubt because it was converted into a house. Its occupants over the years clearly did not mind the sound of passing trains. Passenger facilities were withdrawn in June 1864, less than three years after the Kirriemuir branch opened. No.57441 paused there on 16th June 1960.

80 feet deep gorge carved by glacial meltwater at the end of the Ice Age. The terminus, again close to the town centre, stood around the 360 feet mark. Although a single platform sufficed once more, Kirriemuir station boasted a particularly fine sandstone building, with transverse gables adding interest to a lengthy and lofty single storey block.

The last new work in Strathmore took place around Newtyle. For a remote rural spot, this area had a very complex succession of tracks and stations. As noted previously, the early lines from Newtyle to Glamis and Coupar Angus closed in 1846-47 so that the Scottish Midland Junction could be built, but the eastern branch from Newtyle to a new station at Meigle Junction reopened in 1848. Meanwhile the Dundee & Newtyle had been taken over by the Dundee & Perth and was subsequently converted to standard gauge. Meigle Junction station closed on 1st August 1861 and was replaced by Meigle, where the Alyth branch began. The Newtyle-Ardler Junction spur (in the Coupar Angus direction) seems to have reopened in 1862, but on a slightly different alignment in places.

Having inherited the Dundee-Newtyle line, the Caledonian decided to bypass Hatton Incline and obtained powers for a deviation in 1864. A line from Newtyle to Meigle opened on 3rd August 1868, flying over the main line and curving back to the north side of Meigle station. The deviation from Pitnappie to Nethermill Junction at Newtyle opened on 31st August 1868, involving a tight 180 degree curve round the hillside west of the village to lose height. A new passenger station was provided towards the northern end of this line and the old Newtyle facilities became goods only. The spur from Newtyle to Meigle Junction closed around the same time. Finally, some confusion was cleared up when Meigle became Alyth Junction and Fullarton was renamed Meigle, on 1st November 1876.

Departures from Strathmore branch termini, Monday to Saturday, summer 1948:

BLAIRGOWRIE
7.30am Dundee West (via Newtyle)
9.30am Dundee West (via Newtyle)
1.15pm SO Dundee West (via Newtyle)
1.30pm SX Dundee West (via Newtyle)
2.40pm SO Dundee West (via Newtyle)
4.33pm Alyth (16 minute stand at Newtyle)
6.25pm Dundee West (via Newtyle)

ALYTH
6.40am Blairgowrie (via Ardler)
5.50pm Alyth Junction

KIRRIEMUIR
7.22am Forfar
10.45am Forfar
2.25pm Forfar
6.25pm Forfar

SO Sats only, SX Sats excepted.

FROM GLORY TO OBLIVION

With the completion of bridge improvements in Strathmore during 1888 and the opening of the Forth Bridge in 1890, rivalry between the Caledonian and North British for Grampian traffic intensified. It was fairly civilised for a few years, but during 1895 the West Coast and East Coast alliances seemed to lose all sense of reason and embarked on a dangerous game for London-Aberdeen supremacy. The races could have resulted in disaster; fortunately they were abandoned before a serious accident occurred.

Bradshaw for summer 1895 showed simultaneous departures from Euston and King's Cross at 8pm, arriving in Aberdeen within a few minutes of each other. But the East Coast companies decided to introduce a smart overnight express, reaching its destination at 7.20am, some twenty minutes ahead of its rival. On 15th July 1895 the West Coast partners speeded up their own service to give a 7am arrival, followed seven days later by an East Coast acceleration resulting in 6.45am finish in Aberdeen. For over a month these trains tore north through Britain, drivers straining to get every ounce of power from their engines. Timetables were abandoned, stranded passengers were picked up by duplicate services in the wake of the expresses and safety, speed restrictions and passenger comfort were completely ignored.

This was bad enough, but on the 20th and 21st August the race got completely out of hand, with reporters from London newspapers on each train. The evening departures on the 20th ran neck and neck, with the Caledonian reaching Kinnaber Junction one minute in front of the North British. With a breakneck effort, the East Coast train was well ahead the next day, covering the 523 miles in 8 hours 32 minutes, an average speed of over 60 mph. However, this involved such madness as crossing the Tay Bridge at 72 mph instead of the mandatory 25 mph. With this, the Great Northern, North Eastern and North British called an end to the antics, but the West Coast companies had a last fling the next day when their train averaged 63 mph. One feature of the races was that the trains were virtually abandoned by ordinary passengers; on the final three days the West Coast services carried a total of just 35 people. Afterwards there was a period when the contestants blamed each other for the reckless behaviour.

Although the West Coast and East Coast routes overall settled down to somewhat steadier schedules after August 1895, the smart running established by the Caledonian was maintained to some extent, especially by fast night expresses. Strathmore continued to be a racing ground and it was the first stretch of railway in Britain where a start to stop average of 60mph appeared in *Bradshaw*. This was by the up West Coast Postal which covered the 32.5 miles from Forfar to Perth in 32 minutes, the fine 'Dunalastair' 4-4-0s maintaining this timing. Generally trains became more luxurious as well. The 'Grampian Express' between Glasgow, Edinburgh and Aberdeen, introduced in 1905, consisted of superb twelve-wheel corridor coaches, resplendent in purple lake and white livery. With an ethereal blue Caley loco at the front, they must have presented a glorious sight in Strathmore against fields, coppices and bronze-grey hills.

At the time, the valley was alive with local trains as well. To quote the late John Thomas, 'In the golden years the main line stopping trains progressed up the strath sending a wash of little chocolate and white trains rippling towards the edge of the valley. Strathmore was a lively place then.' In the opposite direction, Blairgowrie trains came down to Coupar Angus, often continuing along the main line to Forfar, or combining with coaches from Alyth to climb over the Sidlaws to Dundee West. Likewise, Kirriemuir trains sometimes terminated at Forfar or joined Brechin portions for the run to Dundee East.

In LMS years, Stanier class 5s replaced most ex-Caledonian tender locos on expresses, although local trains remained largely in the hands of reliable 0-4-4Ts of pre-grouping design. However, bus services increasingly affected patronage and if it had not been for World War 2, the branches may well have closed to passengers in the 1940s. In fact the system remained intact into early BR days, the only casualties having been Kirriemuir Junction in June 1864 and Newtyle old station in August 1868. The picture changed rapidly over a five year period. Passenger trains on the Alyth branch ceased on 2nd June 1951, followed by those to Kirriemuir on 4th August 1952. Closure of the Ardler Junction spur in March 1952 resulted in complicated shunting movements at Alyth Junction for Blairgowrie-Dundee West trains. These finished on 10th January 1955 and most local trains on the main line ceased on 11th June 1956, resulting in the closure of Ardler, Eassie and Glamis. As a finale to this first phase of decline, 5th May 1958 saw the end of goods traffic between Newtyle and Auchterhouse.

Following the Beeching report, retrenchment resumed with the withdrawal of goods facilities at Newtyle and Jordanstone on 7th September 1964. The following year saw the end of all three branches to the northern side of the valley. Alyth and Meigle depots closed on 25th January 1965, Kirriemuir goods - together with Ardler yard on the main line - went on 21st June 1965, and Blairgowrie finished on 6th December 1965, as did Glamis yard. Eassie goods closed on 28th March 1966, although a private siding lasted for another sixteen years.

Main line passenger services had received a boost on 18th June 1962 when the three-hour Glasgow-Aberdeen expresses were resurrected, Gresley A4 Pacifics providing impressive motive power on most trains. These were the last 60mph timings for steam traction on a regular basis, and they attracted enthusiasts from all over Britain. So when No.60024 KINGFISHER powered the 08.25 from Glasgow Buchanan Street to Aberdeen for the last time on 14th September 1966, it was a sad occasion. Apart from one working, through freight was diverted via Dundee on 3rd April 1967. The very last passenger service was on 3rd September 1967, Coupar Angus, Alyth Junction and Forfar stations closed, and the racing ground was no more. Goods traffic from Forfar, Eassie and Coupar Angus to Perth continued, two trains at a time, the branch closing on 7th June 1982.

The splendid finale of Strathmore expresses. A4 Pacific No.60024 KINGFISHER calls at Coupar Angus with the 13.30 Aberdeen-Glasgow Buchanan Street on 29th August 1966. Gangers stand back, a few passengers wait to board, and enthusiasts in the first coach soak up the swansong of these mighty engines.

Above. **In a heavy shower on 17th September 1958, Mogul No.42800 passes St. Leonards Bridge box with the 11.20am from Inverness to Edinburgh Waverley, having replaced class 5 4-6-0 No.45470 at Perth. Meanwhile D11 4-4-0 No.62674 FLORA MACIVOR backs down for the 4.20pm to Glasgow Queen Street via the Devon Valley. Perth carriage and wagon works is in the middle distance, while Moncreiffe Hill forms a damp misty skyline.**

Below. **On 18th June 1962, the first day of the new three-hour service, Gresley A4 Pacific No.60011 EMPIRE OF INDIA storms away from Perth with the 7.10am 'Bon Accord' from Aberdeen to Glasgow Buchanan Street. Unfortunately this inaugural train was 16 minutes late, the loco having been detached to take water. The express had been routed into the down through platform, which did not have a water column at its southern end.....**

CHAPTER 5
PERTH

From the late 1840s Perth was served by trains from four directions and became one of the most important railway centres in Britain as more lines were opened over the ensuing half century. It boasted the busiest main line interchange station in Scotland and apart from a couple of temporary platforms and modest local facilities at Princes Street near the River Tay, the city has only ever had one station. In its final form, Perth General was an enormous, busy and sometimes hectic place. Its four through platforms and five bays were approached by just three sets of tracks - from the north, south and east - but by means of major junctions a few miles outside the city, traffic flowed in from no less than twelve trunk, cross-country and branch lines.

Compared with places such as Carlisle, York, Crewe and Derby, which also became nodal points on the railway system at an early date, Perth was hampered by difficult topography - or so a cursory examination might suggest. The wide Tay and its even broader estuary were obstacles to railway construction, although the valley clearly made a natural routeway. To the north and west the Grampians and West Highlands stretched away for over 70 miles and often rose to well over 3,000ft, presenting a daunting barrier. A thick pile of volcanic rock forming the Sidlaw Hills pointed towards Perth from the north east and came right down to the Tay at Kinnoull Hill. Another mass of ancient lava made up the Ochil Hills, a 35 mile east-west ridge almost cutting off Perth from the Central Lowlands. If this was not enough, abruptly rising ground immediately south of the city culminated in Kirkton Hill and Moncreiffe Hill.

PUMPING STATION

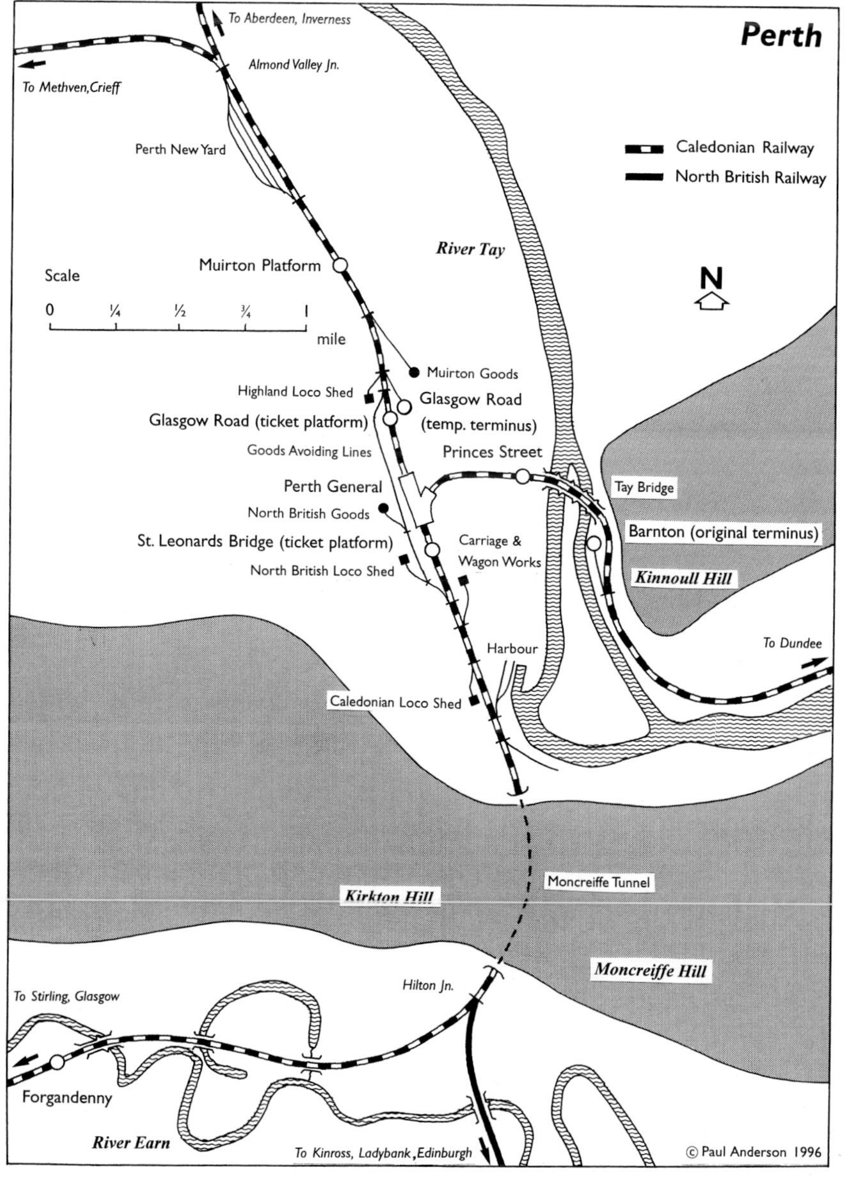

However, Perth owes an enormous debt to the Ice Age. Glaciers and glacial meltwater gouged clefts, deep valleys and great hollows out of the rocks, creating a whole series of relatively straightforward passages through the hills. From Perth, such routeways radiated out in each of the eight main compass directions, and all but one of them was followed by a railway. The resultant system is too much to incorporate in one chapter, so attention will be largely confined to General Station, leaving Chapters 6, 7 and 8 to examine the approaches in detail. Nevertheless, at least a broad outline of the various lines is necessary to provide the background.

THE ROUTES

East of Perth the Tay estuary begins to swell out below the Sidlaw foothills. At first there is only a narrow thread of low ground at the base of Kinnoull Hill, but this soon widens out to form the Carse of Gowrie. In 1847 the Dundee & Perth Railway utilised this favourable terrain to reach Barnhill (Chapter 1) although it was two years before a bridge was built to take the line across the river and actually into Perth. South west of the city, Strathearn provided a convenient passage between Gask Ridge and the Ochill Hills. Beyond a 500ft watershed at Gleneagles, Strathallan formed a vital gap between the Ochils and 2,000ft Creag Beinn and led to Dunblane, Stirling and the Forth-Clyde valley. This important route was followed by the Scottish Central Railway in 1848, although to reach it a tunnel was required under Moncreiffe Hill.

South east of Perth there was a certain amount of flat ground around the mouth of the River Earn and on the south bank of the Tay, but Ormiston Hill brought the Ochills almost to high water mark at Newburgh. East of here, Lindores Gap gave access to the Howe of Fife, Cupar

On 24th July 1965 BR Standard class 6 Pacific No.72008 CLAN MACLEOD waited impatiently to take the 20.25 Perth - London Euston as far as Carlisle. The departure was allocated platform No.6. Adjoining bay No.5 was occupied by an English Electric diesel on another southbound train.

and Kirkcaldy. The Edinburgh & Northern Railway came this way from Burntisland in 1848, joining the Scottish Central at Hilton Junction just south of Moncreiffe Tunnel. North east of the city, Strathmore afforded an easy passage between the Sidlaw Hills and the Grampians. As described in Chapter 4, it was used by the Scottish Midland Junction Railway, also in 1848.

That concluded the post-mania schemes which put Perth firmly on the railway map. North west of the city, Strath Tay extends into the mountains and was tentatively explored by a branch to Dunkeld in 1856. However, there is also a way through to Inverness via the Pass of Killiecrankie, Glen Garry, the Pass of Druimuachdar and Strath Spey. This was the route taken by the Inverness & Perth Junction Railway, completed in 1863 and soon to become the Highland Railway. Branches to Aberfeldy and Bankfoot followed in 1865 and 1906 respectively.

West of Perth, the Pow Valley led to Crieff, with Strathearn, Glen Ogle and the Pass of Brander providing access to the Argyll coast. A modest branch from Almond Valley Junction to Methven, just a few miles from the city, opened in 1858. Eight years later this was extended to Crieff which had already been reached by a branch from Gleneagles in 1856. From Crieff, further extensions between 1893 and 1905 took the line to Comrie, St. Fillans and the earlier Callander & Oban Railway near Balquhidder.

So, in less than twenty years six important lines radiated out of Perth, four of them having been completed in the first two years, and three of these opening within a three month period during 1848. Routes to the north and south remained devoid of track however.

South of the city the narrow wooded cleft of Glenfarg cuts through the Ochill Hills. Glenfarg had featured in two abortive schemes during the 1840s but did not gain its main line until 1890. This was the cut-off between Mawcarse (on the local route between Ladybank, Kinross and Cowdenbeath) and Bridge of Earn on the former Edinburgh & Northern line. It was one of the improvements associated with the Forth Bridge. From 1909 a certain amount of traffic also flowed in from the North Fife line which ran between St. Fort and Newburgh.

Finally, north of Perth, there are ways through the Grampians to Braemar, Ballater and Deeside via Glen Shee, Glen Ardle or Glen Tilt. It would have been difficult to build lines along any of these, and the traffic potential was very low. A branch extended as far as Blairgowie at the beginning of Glen Shee (Chapter 4) whilst Blair Atholl on the Highland line served as a railhead for Glen Tilt, but nothing further was contemplated.

Perth motive power depot allocation 1955:

Class	No.
Jubilee 4-6-0	3
Stanier Class 5 4-6-0	62
Standard Class 5 4-6-0	5
Compound 4-4-0	2
Ex-Caledonian 4-4-0	8
Ex-North British D34 4-4-0	2
Fairburn 2-6-4T	2
Standard 2-6-4T	1
Ex-Caledonian 0-4-4T	5
Hughes/Fowler 2-6-0	1
Fowler 0-6-0	8
Ex-Caledonian 0-6-0	1
Ex-Caledonian 0-6-0T	7

GENERAL STATION

With a population of some 23,000 and widely regarded as the 'gateway to the Highlands', Perth was clearly a major goal for railways in the 1840s. Initially, this enthusiasm was not generally reciprocated locally. The town was sensitive about its harbour which was the focus of trade, despite being tidal and lacking scope for expansion. Early quests for a station site were met with hostility and Perth had to wait until the 1880s before passenger facilities worthy of this important junction were provided.

The Dundee & Perth Railway wanted to build its terminus on South Inch, an area of parkland immediately south of the town, but there were loud protests from nearby residents about the threatened desecration of a much-loved open space. The company itself had doubts

There was plenty of interest from local youngsters as Britannia Pacific No.70007 COEUR-DE-LION arrived at Perth on 3rd April 1965 with the 06.05 parcels from Carlisle. A Birmingham RCW diesel stands at the head of a rake of coaches in the carriage sidings and the villas and terraces of Glover Street form a backdrop.

because of the difference in level between South Inch and the proposed Tay bridge. In the event they settled for temporary facilities at Barnhill on the opposite side of the river, pending construction of the viaduct. Scottish Central metals were the first to reach Perth and a simple two-platform station opened on 23rd May 1848, a little way west of the existing built up area. By the following September this had to accommodate Edinburgh & Northern trains from Burntisland and Scottish Midland Junction services from Forfar, Arbroath and Montrose. The Dundee line was extended across the Tay in 1849, a reversal being necessary to gain access to the station. Workings from Aberdeen added yet more traffic in 1850 and by this time Perth had begun to embrace its new transport role with enthusiasm.

Space had to be found for local trains from Methven and Dunkeld in the 1850s, although the latter used a separate terminus on Glasgow Road for a while during a dispute (see Chapter 6). With impending completion of the Highland line from Inverness, something had to be done to sort out the worsening congestion and inevitable conflicts between the various companies converging on Perth. The outcome was Perth General Station Joint Committee, set up in 1863. Matters were simplified with the amalgamations of 1865/66 which left the Caledonian, North British and Highland as partners. In 1865 meanwhile, the station was rebuilt, with new curving platforms for the Dundee line.

Traffic levels continued to increase relentlessly and during the early 1880s the Joint Committee decided to remodel Perth General on a massive scale, creating the impressive facilities largely intact today. The main feature was a huge island platform with a 1,415ft face for down (northbound) services and a 1,672ft side for up (southbound) trains. These were Nos. 7 and 4 respectively although by the early 1920s the northern end of the latter had became No. 10. At the north end were two bays mainly for Highland, Methven and Crieff locals (Nos. 8 and 9) whilst the southern end had bays for Glasgow, Edinburgh and Fife services (Nos. 5 and 6). The curved Dundee platforms were designated Nos 1 and 2. Hotel platform No. 3 was also a bay and saw much use for marshalling purposes, although some timetabled services commenced there as well.

Refreshment and waiting rooms together with booking, parcels and luggage offices, were accommodated in a succession of buildings on the island platform. These were sturdily constructed in sandstone and displayed strong Tudor styling. Two large projecting clocks hurried passengers along. Most of the station was sheltered by an overall roof consisting of a mixture of transverse and longitudinal gables with decorative end screens reminiscent of Dundee West and Edinburgh Princes Street. Conventional 'ridge and furrow' canopies supported by iron columns were provided on the Dundee platforms. Pedestrian access was by way of a wide footbridge from the main entrance off Leonard Street and a stairway also led down from St. Leonards Road bridge at the south end of the station. Glasgow Road spanned the rails just north of the station and a roadway carried on a viaduct led from it, providing a way down to the platforms for cabs and mail vans.

A station hotel was proposed as early as 1865, although it did not materialise until 1890. Owned by the Joint Committee and located opposite the main entrance, it was a splendid example of Scottish baronial architecture. Fine Tudor windows, somewhat more gothic than those in the station itself, broke up the dour three-storey facade of rough-hewn sandstone, whilst the skyline was a romantic display of conical and hexagonal turrets, stepped gables and tall chimneys. It gained a reputation for efficiency and comfort, and was often patronised by royalty in Edwardian times.

A three-road carriage shed stood just outside the western wall of the station and through goods lines passed by the far side of this lengthy structure. Beyond here was the North British goods depot. The Caledonian had yards north

A4 Pacific No.60007 SIR NIGEL GRESLEY leaves Perth for Carstairs on 24th May 1965 with the up postal, which had left Aberdeen at 3.30pm. The former North British engine shed, closed in December 1949, can be seen on the right next to the new signalling centre. Perth South shed, the rebuilt Caledonian establishment, was in front of misty Kirkton hill in the background.

On 28th May 1960 A1 Pacific No.60159 BONNIE DUNDEE leaves Perth with the 8.20am from Inverness to Edinburgh Waverley. The leading vehicle is a 'Blue Spot' insulated fish van. Two Jubilees on the 12.10pm to Euston were waiting at platform 3 off to the right.

and south of Perth General, at Elibank Street and Friarton respectively. Each of the pre-grouping companies had its own engine shed in the city, at Friarton (Caledonian), Glasgow Road (Highland) and St. Leonards (North British). Traffic was controlled by four signal boxes. St. Leonards and Glasgow Road cabins were positioned at the station approaches, whilst Up Centre and Down Centre boxes were actually on the island platform.

TRAFFIC

Perth enjoyed the benefits of main line services from the outset. In 1848 trains began to run to Stirling and Glasgow, with through journeys to Carlisle and London a vast improvement on the stagecoaches. It also became relatively easy to reach Edinburgh by means of the Edinburgh & Northern Railway and the Burntisland - Granton ferry. Aberdeen - Euston expresses began to pass through Perth in 1850 and Inverness services stated in 1863. Fast trains to Edinburgh via the Forth Bridge commenced in 1890 and through coaches continued on East Coast expresses to King's Cross. Tourist traffic to places such as Crieff and Aberfeldy also thrived. The most eminent tourist was Queen Victoria who favoured Perth General's dining room for breakfast on her outward journey to Balmoral, and took tea there on the way back to London.

By Edwardian times Perth was well established as a major interchange for main line and local traffic. For instance, in 1904 a Highland express arrived at 7pm and within an hour or so there were connections for Dundee, Crieff, Ladybank, Forfar, Glasgow Buchanan Street and Queen Street, Edinburgh Waverley and Princes Street and London Euston, King's Cross and St. Pancras. The heaviest departure in this procession was the 8pm to Euston which usually had two Caledonian 'Dunalastair' 4-4-0s in charge. Highland and North British locos of the same wheel arrangement dominated principal trains on the Inverness and Edinburgh routes respectively, whilst 0-4-4 tanks operated most local services out of Perth. The station had a particularly hectic time during the fortnight preceding August 12th - the 'Glorious Twelfth' when grouse shooting began. A contemporary novel summed up the Perth stationmaster at this time: 'untiring, forceful, ubiquitous ... presiding over a scene of excitement and confusion.'

Goods traffic was also prolific at Perth. Fish wagons were attached to southbound trains and an overnight express fish to London passed through. Young Highland sheep from the upland farms of Argyll and Perthshire were brought down to the mild wintering grounds of Tayside. The city was also an important centre for horse sales, which took place on Fridays and the second Monday of each month. There were also incoming raw materials and outgoing finished products associated with Perth's domestic industries - dyeing, tanning, iron founding, engineering, brewing and whisky blending. Although railways hastened the decline of Perth as a port, a certain amount of coastal shipping continued and justified a branch down to the harbour. This was opened by the Scottish Central as early as 1852.

During World War I Perth station took on a very special role. On 7th August 1914, three days after the conflict began, local women took pity on tired and hungry soldiers waiting for trains in the small hours and gave them tea and cakes. This spontaneous gesture gave rise to a massive operation involving two hundred volunteers and dedicated rooms in the station and hotel. The 'Free Buffet' movement came into its own between February 1917 and April 1919 when the daily Euston - Thurso 'Naval Specials' ran. Troops bound for the northern bases of the Grand Fleet had to endure a 717 mile journey, of 21 hours, with no refreshments on board. Of the ten intermediate stations providing sustenance, Perth was especially impor-

A3 Pacific No.60096 PAPYRUS draws into the up through platform at Perth with the 5.15pm 'Granite City' Aberdeen - Glasgow Buchanan Street express on 27th April 1963. The fireman is dropping off to operate the water crane. Prominent on the right are the curving Dundee platforms.

Departures from Perth, Monday to Saturday, Summer 1948:
SO - Saturdays only
SX - Saturdays excepted
MO - Mondays only
MX - Mondays excepted
MFO - Mondays and Fridays only
MSO - Mondays and Saturdays only
TC - Through carriages

12.53am	MO Aberdeen (ex-Glasgow Buchanan Street)
1.00am	MX Aberdeen (ex-Glasgow Buchanan Street)
1.10am	MX Inverness (ex-Glasgow Buchanan Street)
1.25am	MO Inverness (ex-Glasgow Buchanan Street)
4.55am	MX Glasgow Buchanan Street (ex-Inverness)
5.05am	Inverness (ex-London Euston)
5.50am	Struan
5.50am	Glasgow Buchanan Street
6.00am	Aberdeen (ex-Glasgow Central)
6.05am	SX Edinburgh Waverley (via Glenfarg TC ex-Inverness)
6.33am	Dundee West
6.42am	Ladybank
6.46am	Inverness
7.00am	Glasgow Buchanan Street
7.05am	Dundee West
7.15am	Aberdeen
7.48am	Crieff (via Gleneagles)
7.52am	Dundee Tay Bridge (via St Fort)
7.57am	Glasgow Queen Street (via Devon Valley)
7.58am	Dundee West
8.13am	Edinburgh Waverley (via Glenfarg)
8.32am	Glasgow Buchanan Street (ex-Dundee West)
8.37am	SO Aberdeen (ex-Glasgow Buchanan Street)
8.45am	Glasgow Buchanan Street (ex-Aberdeen)
8.55am	London Euston
9.10am	Edinburgh Waverley (via Glenfarg)
9.12am	Dundee West (ex-Glasgow Buchanan Street)
9.20am	Aberdeen (ex-Glasgow Buchanan Street)
9.25am	Ladybank
9.38am	Blair Atholl
10.00am	Crieff (via Methven Junction)
10.00am	Glasgow Buchanan Street
10.06am	SO Aberdeen (ex-Glasgow Buchanan Street)
10.20am	Dundee West
10.58am	Dundee West (ex-Glasgow Buchanan Street)
11.20am	SO Glasgow Buchanan Street (ex-Aberdeen)
11.25am	Montrose (ex-Edinburgh Princes Street)
11.38am	Aberdeen (ex-Glasgow Buchanan Street)
11.47am	Dundee West
11.55am	Inverness (ex-Glasgow Buchanan Street)
12.01pm	Glasgow Buchanan Street (ex-Aberdeen)
12.05pm	SO Inverness
12.10pm	Inverness (ex-Glasgow Buchanan Street)
12.15pm	London Euston
12.22pm	Glasgow Buchanan Street (ex-Dundee West)
12.25pm	Edinburgh Waverley (via Glenfarg)
12.30pm	Crieff (via Methven Junction)
12.30pm	SO Glasgow Buchanan Street (ex-Stonehaven)
12.39pm	Ladybank
12.41pm	SO Aberdeen (ex-Glasgow Buchanan Street)
12.45pm	SO Glasgow Buchanan Street (ex-Aberdeen)
1.05pm	SO Dundee Tay Bridge (via St. Fort)
1.07pm	Dundee West
1.39pm	SO Aberdeen (ex-Glasgow Buchanan Street)
1.40pm	Falkirk Grahamston
1.50pm	SO Dundee West
2.30pm	SO Glasgow Buchanan Street (ex-Aberdeen)
3.00pm	SO Glasgow Buchanan Street (ex-Inverness)
3.20pm	Glasgow Buchanan Street (ex-Inverness)
3.21pm	Aberdeen (ex-Glasgow Buchanan Street)
3.27pm	Edinburgh Waverley (via Glenfarg TC ex-Inverness)
3.32pm	Dundee West (ex-Glasgow Buchanan Street)
3.40pm	Dundee Tay Bridge (via St. Fort)
3.40pm	SO Inverness (ex-Glasgow Buchanan Street)
3.45pm	SO Glasgow Buchanan Street (ex-Montrose)
3.45pm	SX Glasgow Buchanan Street (ex-Aberdeen)
3.54pm	SX Gleneagles
3.55pm	SO Glasgow Buchanan Street (ex-Aberdeen)
4.00pm	Ladybank
4.00pm	Inverness (ex-Glasgow Buchanan Street)
4.10pm	Dundee West
4.10pm	Blair Atholl
4.15pm	SO Edinburgh Waverley (via Glenfarg)
4.17pm	Crieff (via Methven Junction)
4.30pm	Glasgow Queen Street (via Devon Valley)
4.30pm	Aberdeen
5.04pm	MSO Glasgow Buchanan Street (ex-Aberdeen)
5.22pm	Crieff (via Methven Junction)
5.27pm	Edinburgh Waverley (via Glenfarg)
5.30pm	Dundee West
5.32pm	Glasgow Buchanan Street (ex-Aberdeen)
5.40pm	Glasgow Buchanan Street
6.02pm	Dundee West
6.05pm	Ladybank
6.15pm	Coupar Angus
6.45pm	Dundee West
6.45pm	Aberdeen (ex-Glasgow Buchanan Street)
6.50pm	Stirling (ex-Crieff via Methven Junction)
7.07pm	MFO Glasgow Buchanan Street (ex-Inverness)
7.15pm	SO Dundee West
7.19pm	SO Glasgow Buchanan Street (ex-Inverness)
7.25pm	Glasgow Queen Street (via Devon Valley)
7.35pm	Glasgow Buchanan Street (ex-Inverness)
7.50pm	Edinburgh Waverley (via Glenfarg TC ex-Inverness)
7.55pm	Dundee West (ex-Glasgow Buchanan Street)
8.00pm	Glasgow Buchanan Street (ex-Aberdeen)
8.10pm	Blair Atholl
8.15pm	London Euston
9.19pm	SO Aberdeen (ex-Glasgow Buchanan Street)
9.45pm	London Euston (ex-Inverness)
9.45pm	Dundee West
10.00pm	SO Glasgow Central (ex-Aberdeen)
10.15pm	SX Glasgow Central

tant. By the time the movement was wound up in June 1919 it had served an estimated 1.5 million servicemen.

Perth station became LMS/LNER joint in 1923, but it was dominated by pre-Grouping main line engines for some years. There were the Highland 'Ben' and 'Loch' 4-4-0s, together with 'Clan' 4-6-0s and the very fine 'Castle' 4-6-0s. Caledonian locos included various classes of 'Dunalastair' 4-4-0s, the huge 'Cardean' 4-6-0s, Pickersgill 2 cylinder and 3 cylinder 4-6-0s and the 'River' 4-6-0s purchased brand new from an embarrassed Highland management. North British 4-4-0s worked the Devon Valley services to Glasgow and Atlantics had powered principal Edinburgh trains via Glenfarg since 1906. The 4-4-2s had to be turned at Perth South shed as the 'table at the North British establishment was not long enough.

At the same time, Perth retained its status as an interchange point without parallel in Britain. Some of the exchanges of rolling stock reached staggeringly complex levels. This is amply illustrated by one example from the summer of 1923. The 10.10am from Glasgow to Inverness (worked by a Highland engine all the way from Buchanan Street) and the 9.56am from Edinburgh Waverley to Inverness (a summer relief which changed engines at Perth) met at General. They proceeded as the 11.55am limited stop via Forres and the 12.05pm semi-fast via Slochd summit respectively. However, both the Glasgow and Edinburgh trains had portions for each Highland route beyond Aviemore. Furthermore, the Pullman luncheon cars had to be correctly marshalled and the Glasgow service had a through coach for Aberfeldy which had to be detached from the rear at Ballinluig!

Some through coaches that summer travelled considerably further. The up Aberdeen and Dundee sleeper, due to leave Perth at 10.05pm, had vehicles for Liverpool (and even Southampton on Thursdays) for trans-Atlantic liner passengers. Overnight trains kept Perth busy in the small hours during 1923. The 12.12am and 12.35am arrivals from Glasgow and Euston respectively continued as the 12.50am for Aberdeen and 1.30am for Inverness. Then came the Highland sleepers from Euston (4.42am arrival) and King's Cross (4.47am arrival) leaving at 4.50am for Inverness and 5.00am for Aberdeen. Engines were changed at Perth and the trains were almost always double headed.

The joint ownership of Perth station, dating back to the mid-1860s, finally came to an end in 1948 when the LMS and LNER became part of British Railways. Despite this unification, passenger services retained much of their pre-grouping character as is evident in the accompanying list of departures for summer 1948. The only absentees were the locals to Methven and Bankfoot which had been withdrawn in the 1930s. On the motive power front it was a different picture. Most Highland locos had long been consigned to the scrapheap, although ex-North British 4-4-0s and 4-4-2Ts often powered stopping trains. Several former Caledonian 4-4-0s and tank classes resided at Perth South shed, but these were outnumbered by LMS types, notably Stanier 5MT 4-6-0s. Allocations for 1955 are shown in the table. The dominance of Black 5s is evident in the following account by W.A.C. Smith who visited Perth on Saturday 4th September 1954.

'I arrived at Perth by the down 'Bon Accord' from Glasgow (1.35pm Buchanan Street - Aberdeen) which comprised Stanier class 5 No.45491 on ten corridors, arriving seven minutes late at 3.17pm because of a signal stop at Dunblane. Standard class 5 No.73007 soon drew in with the Dundee portion of the 1.45pm from Buchanan Street, the train having been divided outside the station at St. Leonards Bridge box, with No.45053 picking up the Inverness coaches. After watching No.44721 arrive with the 1.15pm Aberdeen - Glasgow and No.44720 come in with the 2.05pm from Edinburgh Waverley, I visited the shed (63A) some three quarters of a mile from the station. Passenger power on view comprised Stanier Pacifics Nos.46211 QUEEN MAUD, 46234 DUCHESS OF ABERCORN and 46252 CITY OF LEICESTER, all from Crewe North, local Jubilees Nos.45692 CYCLOPS and 45727 INFLEXIBLE, Carlisle Kingmoor's No.45729 FURIOUS, seventeen Stanier class 5s, a Standard class 5, an Edinburgh St. Margarets B1, a pair of D49s from Dundee and Stirling respectively, D11 No.62676 JONATHAN OLDBUCK from Eastfield, six Pickersgill 4-4-0s and a derelict Compound 4-4-0. Also present were a WD 2-8-0 from St. Margarets, a Forfar

There were plenty of passengers waiting to board the 14.00 Dundee Tay Bridge - Glasgow Buchanan Street at Perth on 21st August 1965. Shedded at Springs Branch Wigan (10A), class 5 4-6-0 No.45390 was running in after a visit to St. Rollox works. The loco had worked the 09.15 from Glasgow to Dundee earlier in the day.

'Crab', a K1 2-6-0 and J36 0-6-0 from Fort William, a Fowler 4F, three Caley 'Jumbos', three 0-6-0Ts and a Dundee Tay Bridge J37.

'Back at the station, Pickersgill 4-4-0 No.54499 left with the 4.00pm to Ladybank and D34 No.62484 GLEN LYON departed with the 4.25pm to Glasgow Queen Street. Jubilee No. 45640 FROBISHER then arrived with a train of vans. The up postal from Aberdeen to Carstairs had No.44980 in charge and the passenger portion for Glasgow was taken on by No.44796. Veteran C16 No.67493 then arrived with the 5.10pm from Dundee West, returning on the 7.15pm. Yet another Black 5, No.44881, powered the 4.25pm from Edinburgh Princes Street, while No.44970 arrived with the 'Saint Mungo' (5.00pm Buchanan Street - Aberdeen), the Dundee portion being brought

Class 5 4-6-0 No.44703 leaves Perth on 24th July 1965 with the 09.25 from Crewe to Aberdeen which it had taken over from Britannia No.70003 JOHN BUNYAN. The approach from Glasgow Road crosses the plate girder bridge on the left.

A4 Pacific No.60019 BITTERN leaves Perth for Aberdeen with the 5.30pm 'Saint Mungo' from Glasgow Buchanan Street on 24th May 1965.

in from St. Leonards Bridge by No.45049. An unbalanced working probably accounted for No.45117 piloting No.54476 on the lightweight 5.15pm local from Blair Atholl. No.54499 then arrived back with the 6.02pm from Ladybank. No.44997 was one minute early at 6.54pm with the 3.20pm Inverness - Edinburgh Waverley which was taken on by B1 No.61398. WD 2-10-0 No.90765 came into the west side yard with a down freight; earlier, K3 No.61879 had been observed on another goods. When Compound No.40924 arrived with the 6.10pm from Dundee West it ran through the station to propel the train into the down side platform so that passengers did not have to cross the footbridge! Nos.45483 and 44801 came in with the 2.05pm from Inverness via Forres, two coaches for Waverley being added to the 7.50pm for Edinburgh headed by A3 No.60097 HUMORIST. The Glasgow portion departed behind No.44999. I returned by the 3.40pm ex Inverness which arrived on time double headed by Nos.45463 and 44977. They were replaced on the eight coaches by No.44881 which made a punctual departure at 7.37pm, to be one minute late at Buchanan Street at 9.13pm.'

Inevitably there has been some rationalisation of facilities at Perth, but the city has not suffered as badly as certain erstwhile rail centres. The Highland shed (Perth North) closed during 1938 when the LMS completely rebuilt Perth South (the former Caledonian depot) with a new building, coaling tower and 70ft turntable. However, the HR shed was still used for storing locos and latterly as an engineers supply depot. The small North British shed closed in December 1949, its staff and pair of D49s being transferred to Perth South. Again the building remained *in situ*. Perth South itself finished with steam on 1st May 1967 and closed completely on 5th October 1969, with subsequent demolition.

Goods facilities have all but disappeared. The former Caledonian Friarton yard, just an unstaffed public delivery siding at the end, closed on 25th January 1965, the harbour branch finished on 16th May 1968, and Earlsdyke coal depot closed on 30th June 1969. The North British yard, 'Perth Central' from 1952, was abandoned on 4th May 1970. Perth Muirton goods finished on 16th May 1983 and the remaining business at Perth North goods was transferred to Perth New Yard on 3rd April 1989. This was authorised under the 1955 Modernisation Plan and partially opened on 7th August 1961. It never realised its full potential and nowadays just a few sidings remain for Railtrack use, although the turntable is handy for visiting steam locos. One of the last vestiges of once prolific private sidings traffic went with the closure of the Rowntree Mackintosh siding on 9th June 1989.

In 1962 the Perth area was resignalled and a new power box commissioned. This development, followed by the retrenchment of freight facilities, meant the end of manual boxes at Glasgow Road Bridge, Centre Up, Centre Down and St. Leonards Bridge in the station area. Dovecotland Junction, Balhousie and Almond Valley Junction north of the station, Edinburgh Road Bridge and Friarton south of the station, and Orchardbank on the Dundee line. During the 1970s the overall roof at Perth General was reduced in length, and in 1983 the hotel was sold off to a private operator. Nevertheless it is still an impressive station, with regular and usually frequent services to Dundee and Aberdeen, Glasgow, Edinburgh and Inverness. The variety of trains has largely gone however with only the 'Highland Chieftain' InterCity 125 from King's Cross to Inverness and the 'Royal Highlander' sleeper from Euston to Inverness relieving the usual diet of class 158 diesel multiple units.

Left. Although Princes Street station in Perth originally had two platforms, the down side facilities were removed in the 1930s. Hughes-Fowler 'Crab' 2-6-0 No 42800 rolls into the city centre station with the 5.45pm from Perth General to Dundee West on 18th May 1957.

Below. The 4.10pm local from Dundee West to Perth crossing the Tay on 12th March 1955 with D49 4-4-0 No 62706 FORFARSHIRE in charge. In this view from Shore Road the ten masonry arches carrying the line across Moncreiffe Island are clearly visible, whilst the large villas of Barnhill cling to the wooded slopes of Kinnoull Hill in the background. The bridge was under repair at the time, hence the lifebelts.

Chapter 6

PERTH - EASTERN AND NORTHERN APPROACHES

The railways heading towards Perth from the east and north east have largely been dealt with in earlier chapters. Here it is only necessary to consider the last few miles of the Dundee & Perth as it left the Carse of Gowrie and squeezed between the Sidlaw Hills and upper Tay estuary, then the remaining section of the Scottish Midland Junction where it descended from Strathmore along the lower Tay valley. The scenery encountered by these two lines is attractive enough, but north of Perth the Grampians close in and the landscape becomes spectacularly beautiful. It was explored tentatively by a local line, the Perth & Dunkeld, then dramatically by a main line, the Highland route to Inverness. Finally, two contrasting branches were built. The railway to Aberfeldy was reminiscent of the trunk route through the mountains whilst Bankfoot acquired a light railway, with characteristics more akin to lines in the lowlands.

FROM DUNDEE AND FORFAR

In chapters 1 and 4 the Dundee & Perth and Scottish Midland Junction were left at Errol and Coupar Angus respectively. Thus far, they had enjoyed a very easy passage across gently undulating or even perfectly flat ground. But both the Carse of Gowrie and Strathmore came to an end some miles away from Perth and railway construction became more problematical. In the case of the Dundee line, there was some flat land - but not much - and finding a passage was made worse by an awkward landowner. Hilly terrain and the need to cross several watercourses, notably the Tay and Almond, were the main difficulties faced by the Scottish Midland Junction. Such obstacles proved far from insurmountable however, and the route

HIGHLAND MONARCH

from Dundee opened on 24th May 1847, followed by that from Forfar on 20th August 1848.

At Errol the Dundee & Perth was still very much in the Carse of Gowrie, although the rampart-like Braes of the Carse which reached 944ft at Pole Hill were closing in ominously. Errol station, a mile north of the village, nearly became a junction. Construction work actually began on a short branch to Inchmichael in the shadow of the Braes. Had the scheme come to fruition it would, no doubt, have been a similar line to that serving Inchture (see Chapter 1) but after a large cutting had been excavated the project was abandoned and the alignment used for a road.

The Dundee-Perth line stayed at about 50 feet above sea level as far as Glencarse, but the ground was becoming less even and several earthworks were required. Beyond here, the Braes encroached with a vengeance and forced the trackbed down to the shoreline. Lord Gray of Kinfauns Castle also influenced matters. He released land on the strict condition that the railway kept to the edge of his property, resulting in a shoreline course all the way to Perth. As a bonus, passengers enjoyed fine views of Balhepburn Island and Sleepless Inch on the far side of the channel, with Moncreiffe Hill rising beyond them. Isolated Kilnfauns station was on this section.

A sweeping curve took the track round the 729ft Kinnoull Hill and past Moncreiffe Island to the terminus at Barnhill. Travellers had to endure an inconvenient mile and a half hike or horse bus journey via Perth Bridge to reach the

Class 5 4-6-0s Nos 44978 and 44999 calling at Ballinluig on 28th May 1960 with the 11.00am from Inverness to Glasgow Buchanan Street and Edinburgh Waverley. Ex-Caledonian 0-4-4T No 55173 in the branch platform on the left had arrived earlier with the connecting service from Aberfeldy.

town centre until the railway was extended across the Tay on 8th March 1849. The new line featured a long single-track timber viaduct which incorporated an iron swing span, allowing river craft a clear passage of 50 feet. Immediately beyond the western bank, the rails passed Perth's elegant Georgian waterworks with its distinctive rotunda, then entered Princes Street station. The remainder of the route avoided cherished South Inch, but had to cross Princes Street, Nelson Street, Scott Street, James Street and King Street on a masonry viaduct. A southwards facing junction was made with the Scottish Central just south of Perth station.

Barnhill terminus closed when the extension opened and its site was later used for carriage sidings. Unfortunately the Tay viaduct seems to have been poorly constructed, for the foundations caused problems from the outset, and a second bridge soon replaced it. This time stone piers supporting plate deck girders were used to span the two Tay channels, with ten arches providing the intervening section on Moncreiffe Island. The opportunity was taken to ease the curve at the Barnhill end, although, perhaps surprisingly, the new structure was still only single track. A swing span giving access to quays upstream was retained.

Scottish Midland Junction trains from Forfar began running to Perth over six months before the Dundee & Perth ventured across the Tay. Construction work had taken just over two years, quite an achievement considering the difficult terrain encountered by the sixteen mile section south west of Coupar Angus. The last vestiges of Strathmore were soon left behind. To the north, the River Isla had widened out and flowed towards its confluence with the Tay; ahead, the main river was about to leave the broad meadows of Murthly and Meikleour for a deeply incised section to Stanley and Luncarty. Not only did the Scottish Midland have to reach the western side of the Tay, but it then had to cope with tributary valleys and the swelling contours between them whilst finding a way down from 200 feet almost to sea level.

The featureless ground enjoyed in Strathmore continued for a couple of miles to Woodside and Burrelton, but by Cargill the line was on a hillside and ran through two fair-sized cuttings. A substantial viaduct carried the tracks high above the Tay to Ballathie on the opposite bank. A steady passage at about 180 feet was maintained as far as Stanley, although a succession of earthworks proved necessary, including a mile long cutting behind the village. The descent proper then began, and continued through Luncarty where viaducts across the Ordie and Shochie Burns were required. Only the River Almond barred the way to Perth and this was spanned by another viaduct. A half mile embankment took the line down to 30 feet where it remained as far as Perth station.

There were six intermediate stations on the Coupar Angus-Perth section at one time or another, namely Woodside (Woodside & Burrelton from October 1905, then Burrelton from September 1927), Cargill, Ballathie (closed to passengers as early as July 1868), Stanley, Strathord (optimistically called Dunkeld Road until February 1857), and Luncarty. Furthermore, three platforms with very different roles existed in the Perth area at various times. Glasgow Road station was a temporary terminus which functioned for a few months before May 1860 during a dispute between the Scottish Central and Scottish North Eastern (which had inherited the Scottish Midland Junction). There was also a ticket checking platform at Glasgow Road which was in use until the 1950s for the non-corridor Blair Atholl locals. Finally, Muirton Platform served St Johnston football ground from 1936 to 1960.

The Perth-Coupar Angus route was an integral part of the main line to Aberdeen for well over a century and shared in every stirring episode from the races to Aberdeen to the swansong of the A4s. Chapters 4 and 5 gave a flavour of the traffic and motive power over the years. But three feeder lines added variety; local trains from Methven and Crieff came in at Almond Valley Junction (see Chapter 7), the Bankfoot branch joined at Strathord (see later), and the Highland main line converged at Stanley (see shortly).

Passenger services were withdrawn from Strathord on 13th April 1931,

Delightful Highland Railway buildings at Pitlochry on 24th June 1961. A perfectly proportioned chalet served the down platform whilst the very ornate main building off to the right even featured stone thistles as finials. Birmingham/Sulzer Type 2 diesels D5346 and D5329 called with the 2.05pm from Inverness to Glasgow Buchanan Street and Edinburgh Waverley.

The rugged nature of the Highland main line was evident at Killiecrankie on 24th June 1961 as class 5 4-6-0s Nos 45171 and 45179 heading the 10.35am Glasgow Buchanan Street - Inverness passed a Metro-Cammell twin forming the 11.18am local from Blair Atholl to Perth. There is just a hint of the elegant Highland station buildings.

Luncarty on 18th June 1951 and Stanley, Cargill and Burrelton on 11th June 1956. The goods yard at Ballathie closed on 7th September 1964, nearly a century after the passenger station, and Strathord followed on 2nd November 1964. Traffic ceased at Stanley and Cargill on 6th December 1965, then Luncarty on 23rd May 1966. Burrelton yard soldiered on until 7th June 1982 when the Forfar-Stanley section closed completely. In 1996 the track between Perth and Stanley was still used by Inverness services, including the daily InterCity 125 and Sleeper.

Trains also continue to run over the Perth and Dundee route, although all intermediate stations at the western end have gone. Passenger facilities were withdrawn from Kinfauns on 2nd January 1950, Glencarse on 11th June 1956 and Princes Street on 28th February 1966, all three stations losing their goods yards in 1964 (27th January, 2nd November and 7th September respectively). Considering its fairly remote location, Errol was a remarkable survivor and only succumbed on 28th September 1985.

HIGHLAND

Dunkeld nestles in a magnificent setting of wooded mountain slopes midway along Strathtay. It is something of a cross-roads, with a route to Blairgowrie via Loch of Lowes and the Lunan valley going off to the north east and Strathbraan providing a way through to Crieff away to the south west. The town is also one of the most ancient settlements in Scotland. It was a residence of Pictish Kings and later a Celtic stronghold, hence its name 'Fort of the Celts'. An abbey was established in 729 AD by monks driven out of Iona by the Norsemen and the magnificent cathedral, now an elegant ruin, was begun in the 12th century. The building was devastated in 1560 as a result of the Reformation, and the town itself was virtually destroyed in 1689 during a savage battle between Highlanders and lowland Cameronians.

By 1835 Dunkeld had a population of almost three thousand and a railway was planned from Perth. However, the latter was indifferent and the Duke of Atholl showed hostility, so nothing materialised. A decade and a half later the Scottish Midland Junction proposed a branch, but this time certain influential residents of Dunkeld became obstructive and the company was forced to abandon its plans. Shortly afterwards a local group was formed to build the line, and this included several gentlemen who had thwarted the Scottish Midland scheme! The Perth & Dunkeld Railway Act was passed on 10th July 1854 and ten years of niggling disputes on all manner of issues commenced.

Deep in the Pass of Killiecrankie on 24th June 1961, a Birmingham/Sulzer Type 2 heads north with the 1.45pm service from Glasgow Buchanan Street to Inverness. The castellated viaduct spanned a cleft where a shelf on the mountain slope was no longer available, and it is easy to understand why this section of the Highland remained single track.

The Blair Atholl South signalman prepares to hand over the single line token to the fireman of Standard 2-6-4T No 80092 as it starts away with the 1.18pm stopping train to Perth on 15th June 1960. In the down platform sister loco No 80093 prepares to bank the 10.18am Edinburgh Waverley-Inverness (hauled by class 5 4-6-0 No 44978) 'up the hill' to Druimuachdar summit.

Initially, arguments centred around the actual course of the eight mile line; even in the 1850s damage to the landscape in such a beautiful valley was a consideration. The route eventually adopted left the Scottish Midland Junction north of Stanley and headed across a gentle ridge within a great sweep of the Tay. At Murthly the line veered west along the southern edge of the valley, keeping well above Murthly Castle and piercing a prominent hill at Byres of Murthly by a 310 yard tunnel. This was a difficult bore through hard rock; water seepage caused problems during construction and persisted after the line opened. Rohallion station, named after a ruined castle high up the hill slope and serving little else, preceded the descent through Birnam Wood to the terminus at Birnam, across the river from Dunkeld. The branch opened on 7th April 1856 after a celebration dinner two days earlier, and was worked by the Scottish Midland Junction.

However, the Perth & Dunkeld was at loggerheads with the Scottish Midland from the outset. For example, the former wanted a station at the junction whilst the latter insisted on one actually in Stanley. Then the larger company complained about the incomplete nature of the line and demanded a larger share of the revenue. These uneasy working arrangements were not helped by the level of usage, about two hundred passengers a day. The Scottish Midland Junction had little interest in the line and when the Scottish North Eastern took over it regarded the Dunkeld branch as a liability. But a glorious role was in store for the line from Stanley Junction as part of the Highland Railway.

A route through the Grampians was first mooted in 1845. The Perth & Inverness Railway was a 'mania' scheme and in some quarters the sanity of those intending to push a line over the roof of Scotland was doubted. Parliament concurred and the submission was thrown out in 1846. But as steam locomotives grew in strength, the proposal became increasingly feasible and the initial plan seemed visionary rather than reckless. As a result the Inverness & Perth Junction Railway acquired its Act in 1861 and work began during October of that year.

From Forres on the Inverness-Aberdeen route, the line climbed over Dava Moor then followed the river Spey to Grantown, Aviemore and Kingussie. Another climb up Glen Truim brought the rails to Druimuachdar summit, 1,484 feet above sea level. The descent was by way of Glen Gairn, Blair Atholl, the pass of Killiecrankie, Pitlochry and the Tummel and Tay valleys to Dunkeld where an end-on junction was made with the Perth & Dunkeld Railway. Construction proceeded remarkably quickly considering the very difficult topography, the line opening in stages during 1863 (Dunkeld to Pitlochry on 1st June, Forres to Aviemore on 3rd August and Aviemore to Pitlochry on 9th September). But the hasty progress was at a cost: there was only single track throughout, some stations had not even been started, and several minor bridges were simply built of timber.

The Inverness & Aberdeen Junction (which owned the route through Forres) began working the Perth & Dunkeld, together with the extension to Pitlochry, on 1st June 1863. This arrangement continued until 9th September when the line was opened in its entirety and Inverness & Perth Junction engines took over. The two Inverness companies merged in 1865 to form the Highland Railway, which also incorporated the Perth & Dunkeld. Single track working often caused chaos in subsequent years and the line was doubled from Blair Atholl to Druimuachdar in 1900-1901.

Difficult ground was encountered within two miles of Dunkeld. First, the River Braan had to be spanned, then a 350 yard tunnel took the track through a spur of Craig Vinean. A fairly easy stretch along the flat floor of Strathtay followed, although another substantial river bridge was required at Dalguise where the line switched to the eastern side of the valley before reaching Guay. Large bridges on the Inverness & Perth Junction were treated very decoratively, the abutments rising as castellated towers which were sometimes linked by an arch over the rails.

Beyond Ballinluig the line followed the River Tummel to Pitlochry, an elegant town generally regarded as the geographi-

McIntosh 0-4-4-T No 55212 at Ballinluig with the 1.02pm to Aberfeldy on 23rd May 1955. Upon departure the train reversed into the loop to pick up three wagons of coal and a goods brake van. Three passenger services each way daily could be worked as mixed trains if required.

cal centre of Scotland. Ahead lay the Pass of Killiecrankie where the River Garry rushes through a deep wooded gorge to join the Tummel. In 1689 this was the dramatic setting for a bloody battle where English troops were defeated by Jacobite Highlanders. The railways also had a battle to get through the Pass of Killierankie. In places there was barely enough room to carve out a ledge on the precipitous slopes and at one point a deep cleft had to be crossed by a ten-arch, 54ft high viaduct. A tunnel of 128 yards as well as several retaining walls were also necessary.

An easier stretch led to Blair Atholl, the last place of any size before the ascent into the mountains. The town is noted for nearby Blair Castle, seat of the Duke of Atholl. This rambling Baronial pile in white stone was begun in 1269 and has seen many royal visitors, from Mary Queen of Scots to Queen Victoria. Blair Atholl itself was transformed by the railway; wealthy families moved in and visitors flocked to the health hydros. A small engine shed was established to house banking engines for Inverness-bound trains. With over eight miles of the seventeen mile climb to Druimuachdar at 1 in 70, these were frequently essential.

Much has been written about the Highland Railway, from locos such as the 'Jones Goods' and Drummond 'Castle' 4-6-0s to harsh winters and huge snowploughs used as battering rams. It would be superfluous to repeat such details here, but a snippet of life on the Highland is worth relating. The company successfully promoted its main line to tourists, but by 1900 motor cars were beginning to erode first class receipts despite the poor state of the highways. So a car carrying service up the long drag to Druimuachdar was inaugurated. *Don't trust your precious tyres to the road* instructed a railway poster. John Thomas related one incident. 'It was a condition of travel that most cars must start their rail journeys with empty petrol tanks. There was an occasion when a porter at Blair Atholl inspected a car by poking a naked light inside. That was one car that did not make the journey. A circular was issued to the staff explaining the volatile propensities of petrol, a spirit with which the working person of the time may not have been familiar'. Needless to say, there is now a huge amount of road traffic between Perth and Inverness - the 'improved' A9 carving a massive scar through the Pass of Killiecrankie.

The Highland main line still has a reasonable passenger service, nine trains each way including the King's Cross InterCity 125 and Euston Sleeper, at the time of writing. Dunkeld, Pitlochry and Blair Atholl stations remain open. Apart from Rohallion, which closed in October 1864, the others survived until relatively recently. Guay lost both passenger and goods facilities on 3rd August 1959, the yards at Killiecrankie and Dalguise closing on 28th October 1963 and 27th January 1964. The withdrawal of stopping passenger trains resulted in the closure of Murthly, Dalguise, Ballinluig and Killiecrankie on 3rd May 1965. Goods facilities at Blair Atholl finished on 7th November 1966, although the sidings at Murthly and Dunkeld lasted until 4th August 1969.

ABERFELDY AND BANKFOOT

Six miles east of magnificent Loch Tay, the River Tay is joined by Urlar Burn which tumbles down the wild slopes of 2,081ft Meall á Choire Chreagaich. The attractive town of Aberfeldy grew up near the confluence as a market centre for this mountainous part of Perthshire. Its strategic importance increased during the 1730s with the construction of one of General Wade's military roads and the associated river bridge is regarded as his finest. In 1739 the *Frecadan Dubh*, or Black Watch, was enrolled nearby with the aim of keeping an eye on the Highlanders.

Aberfeldy had a population of almost 7,000 in 1800, although it has declined relentlessly ever since, and now has a mere 1,500 residents. A century and a half ago the town was important enough to attract the attention of early railway developers and may well have been served by the locally promoted Strathtay & Breadalbane Railway which acquired its Act in 1846. When the original Inverness-Perth proposal was rejected, the Aberfeldy scheme became dormant however. The town's distilleries and woollen mill remained a potentially lucrative source of traffic, and a decade or so later the Scottish North Eastern considered a branch, but this was condemned as too costly. Matters became much easier when the Inverness & Perth Junction was sanctioned in 1861, and the line to Aberfeldy finally became a reality.

Although just nine miles in length, the railway from Ballinluig was an expensive undertaking involving 41 bridges, including two major river crossings near the junction. Overall the ascent was negligible - from 220 feet at Ballinluig to 320 feet at the terminus - but unfavourable terrain from Grandtully to Aberfeldy demanded numerous short climbs, often followed by dips, and there was a continuous succession of sharp curves, cuttings and embankments for two thirds of the route. This difficult passage stemmed from the twisting, gorge-like nature of the Tay valley between Aberfeldy and Strathtay proper. Despite the hardships, there seems to have been an excellent working relationship between the contractor and his workforce, the navvies being given generous measures of whisky following completion of the largest cutting!

Once the construction headaches were over, Scotland gained one of its most scenic branch lines, services commencing on 3rd July 1865. The single track curved westwards from Ballinluig and within a mile crossed both the Tummel and Tay on lattice girder bridges with castellated abutments. A fairly easy section on low embankments above the Tay flood plain led the rails to Balnagaurd, but after Sketewan a steep shoulder came right down to the river and hinted at the type of country ahead. At Grandtully the twists and turns began, passengers enjoying superb views of the glistening Tay, except where dense woodland and rock cuttings intervened. On the opposite bank ham-

Balnaguard Halt, between Ballinluig and Grandtully, was opened by the LMS in 1935. It is seen here on 28th May 1960 with the wooded lower slopes of Creag Maoiseach forming a backdrop.

lets and isolated farms clung to the lower slopes of a mighty ridge culminating in the desolate crags of 2,581ft Meall Tairneachan.

Aberfeldy terminus only had a single platform, but the actual building was truly delightful. It was a squat affair in local stone, with twin pavilions featuring crow-stepped gables overlooking a stubby canopy. A goods yard, transit shed, tiny loco shed and water tank completed the layout. Grandtully station had a simple timber structure on its solitary platform, but Balnaguard Halt (opened by the LMS in 1935) could only manage an open fronted shed. The branch led to the establishment of more distilleries alongside the Tay, including that at Grandtully - often quoted as the smallest in Scotland. It also stimulated tourism, and by 1894 Aberfeldy was being described as a 'favourite summer resort'.

In its very early days the branch was worked by tender locos, but 4-4-0Ts - including the distinctive 'Yankee' tanks - soon took over. Under the LMS, ex-Caledonian 0-4-4Ts became the norm, and this situation continued until 1961/62 when BR Standard 2-6-4Ts were introduced. For the last few years Type 2 diesels were an incongruous sight on the one-coach trains. The Aberfeldy branch missed its centenary by exactly two months. Passenger services were withdrawn on 3rd May 1965, goods facilities having finished earlier in the year on 25th January.

Bankfoot is a small town some eight miles north of Perth. Besides being a pleasant place in its own right, it enjoys an attractive setting below the twin peaks of Craig Gibbon and Obney Hills. Although the main road from Perth to Dunkeld passed this way, the railway swung well to the east, through Murthly, and Bankfoot had to wait half a century for its own branch. The Bankfoot Light Railway opened on 1st May 1906, climbing steadily for three miles up the Ordie Burn and Garry Burn valleys from a junction with the Highland main line at Strathord.

Construction was an easy task through the gently rolling agricultural land and earthworks were minimal. A scattering of farmsteads bordered the track, but no intermediate stations were provided. From just over 100 feet above sea level at Strathord the branch passed Marlehall, Newmill and Westwood, reaching 200 feet near Loak. A final uphill stretch brought the line to 260 feet at the terminus. This consisted of one passenger platform with a modest yet attractive single storey timber building, a loading bank, a small wooden goods shed, and three sidings. It was a picturesque site, overlooked by the square tower of the parish church peering down from a low hill.

A reasonable passenger service, sometimes consisting of mixed trains, was provided for a quarter of a century. In 1928 for instance, there were departures at 8.05am (for Strathord), 9.10am (Perth), 12.58pm, 4.15pm, 5.05pm (all Strathord) and 6.18pm (Perth). The Strathord workings connected with main line stopping trains at the junction. On Saturdays nine services were provided, all but three of them through to Perth, and the last departure was a 9.15pm. However, the Bankfoot branch was very vulnerable to bus competition and passenger facilities were withdrawn on 13th April 1931. However, livestock specials continued to be a feature of the line, and seasonal potato traffic was buoyant until the end. The goods yard finally closed on 7th September 1964, resulting in the demise of the branch.

Birmingham/Sulzer Type 2 D5336 at Grandtully on 18th June 1962 with the 10.46am from Ballinluig to Aberfeldy. The coach is an ex-LMS Stanier corridor brake composite, as was the norm in steam days.

With the slopes of Beinn Eagagach forming a magnificent background, BR/Sulzer Type 2 D5123 and a solitary Thompson non-corridor brake composite forming the 4.10pm from Aberfeldy to Ballinluig skirt the sylvan River Tay near Grandtully on 3rd April 1965. This loco and coach combination was standard towards the end, in this case a month before the service ceased

Above. **A down freight with K3 2-6-0 No 61879 in charge emerges from the impressive northern portal of Moncreiffe tunnel and approaches Perth on 4th September 1954. Rural country around the hamlets of Scoonieburn and Tarsappie provided a sylvan setting, but industry and suburbs dominated the view behind the camera.**

Below. **A deep cutting through volcanic rock marked the southern approach to Moncreiffe tunnel. This Park Royal railbus forming the 3.05pm from Stirling to Perth via the Devon Valley on 28th May 1960 has just joined the main Glasgow line at Hilton Junction.**

CHAPTER 7

PERTH - WESTERN APPROACHES

The low lying meadows of Strathearn and the Pow Water valley, sepa rated by the Gask ridge, stretch for fifteen miles west of Perth. On three sides they are surrounded by mountains, like a giant claw about to nip Perth. To the north and west the Grampian flanks reach 3,048ft at Ben Conzie and 3,224 feet at Ben Vorlich, whilst the Ochil Hills culminate in 2,363 feet Ben Cleuch to the south. There are ways out of this great amphitheatre, via the narrow passes of Glen Eagles and Sma' Glen, or alongside Loch Earn. More significant is broad Strathallan, where the Ochils merge with the Highlands and this was the route taken by the Scottish Central Railway from Larbert, Stirling and Dunblane to Perth.

Crieff nestles in the north west corner of the lowlands where the River Earn ceases to be a mountain river and begins its meandering course down to the Tay. With a population approaching three thousand in the early 1800s the town was almost as important as Perth, and until 1770 it was the site of one of Scotland's great 'Trysts' or cattle markets, where drovers from the Highlands met buyers from the south. Crieff wanted a railway from the outset, but it had to build a branch itself. The line from Crieff Junction (eventually Gleneagles) on the Scottish Central was a wonderfully amateurish affair until the Caledonian pulled it into shape. Later, another branch headed along the Pow Water valley from Perth to Crieff, although this only reached Methven at first. Eventually rails were pushed further west, initially to Comrie, then on through increasingly wild country to St Fillans and Lochearnhead.

SCOTTISH CENTRAL

The 57 miles of track from Greenhill (in the Forth valley west of Falkirk) to Perth was another product of the Railway Mania. At the time of its promotion, critics dismissed the scheme as a recipe for commercial failure, predicting that a lengthy line from an empty field to a sedate port across sparsely settled country would attract little traffic. True, much of the Scottish Central route passed through Strathallan and Strathearn where there were few settlements of any size, but Larbert, Stirling, Dunblane and Auchterarder were intermediate places of some significance. Furthermore, the Caledonian was about to forge northwards from Carlisle and Glasgow to the said empty field and the Scottish Midland

Having called at Perth and negotiated Moncreiffe tunnel, A2 Pacific No 60528 TUDOR MINSTREL storms past Hilton Junction with the 09.30 express from Aberdeen to Glasgow Buchanan Street on 21st August 1965. The small building on the right was probably the original signal box controlling converging Scottish Central and Edinburgh & Northern routes to Perth.

BR/Sulzer type 2 No D5125 guides the 11.15 from Glasgow Buchanan Street to Dundee past Hilton Junction box on 21st August 1965. In this panoramic view from Craigend near the southern portal of Moncreiffe tunnel, the wooded ridge at Forgandenny rises above Strathearn in the middle distance, the Ochil Hills forming a brooding skyline.

Junction had plans to carry the rails forward through Strathmore towards Aberdeen. The promoters proved to be men of foresight, for their railway soon became a trunk route.

Parliamentary approval for the Scottish Central came in 1845, construction work being entrusted to the renowned contractor Thomas Brassey. Perth industrialists were quite excited by the project as it would speed up the delivery of raw materials to their textile factories. Furthermore, with 8,000 men employed on building the Scottish Central and Scottish Midland Junction at one stage, many local residents were very much aware that a transport revolution was taking place. Passenger services between Greenhill and Stirling began on 3rd March 1848 and were extended to Perth on 23rd May 1848. The ten mile connection with the Glasgow-Carlisle line was opened by the Caledonian Railway on 7th August 1848.

The Scottish Central soon proved a great success and traffic grew steadily, especially after Aberdeen-London trains began to use it in 1850. In fact, its dividend of 7 per cent was the second highest in Scotland. However, the motive power policy was a little chaotic at first. Fifteen 2-2-2s were ordered for the opening of the line, but as the date grew closer concern was expressed that this would not be enough. More were ordered, bringing the total to 45. When trains began running, the company found it had *too many* engines and tried to sell or hire some out, but there was a glut of motive power in Scotland at the time. As traffic increased, the surplus was in turn taken up and yet more had to be ordered!

From just above sea level at Perth the line climbed to 430 feet near Blackford, eighteen miles away, with most of the ascent taking place in the last seven miles. After passing Friarton, just south of Perth, the Scottish Central was faced with the ridge culminating in Kirkton Hill (540ft) and Moncreiffe Hill (725ft). Although the ground dipped to 200 feet between these summits, a bore through the tough volcanic whinstone was inevitable. Moncreiffe tunnel, 1,215 yards between portals and the longest in northern Scotland, was curved and had three smoke vents. The line emerged in a sheer rock cutting, but soon entered eastern Strathmore, still just above sea level. A lengthy embankment carrying the rails above the flood plain was punctuated by two bridges across an ox-bow lake (an abandoned loop of the river) then a 520ft long twenty-two arch viaduct across the Earn itself.

Forgandenny station (4 miles from Perth) followed, then the line passed through two long cuttings through glacial debris on the valley side. Just before Forteviot (7 miles) the line spanned Water of May which had just left its wooded

On a sunny Whit Saturday afternoon, 28th May 1966, class 5 4-6-0 No 44794 hurries past former Auchterarder station with the 13.30 Aberdeen-Glasgow Buchanan Street. Craig Rossie, reaching 1,349 feet, towers above Strathearn a couple of miles away.

Gleneagles station, with its informative nameboard, on 12th March 1955. Class 5 4-6-0 No 45470 headed the 11.35am Dundee West to Glasgow Buchanan Street. Being a Saturday, the restaurant car train had been strengthened by a pair of non-corridor coaches!

gorge, having drained a large area of the Ochils below Slungie Hill. The railway finally climbed above 50 feet at Forteviot and reached 100 feet at Dunning (nearly 10 miles) before curving towards the hills and leaving Strathearn well to the north. The climb then began in earnest : 150 feet at Aberuthyen; 200 feet at Shinafoot; 250 feet at Coul; 300 feet just after Auchterarder (14 miles).

Another viaduct strode across the deep cleft formed by Ruthven Water, rushing down from Gleneagles to Strathearn. Gleneagles station (Crieff Junction at first and not opened until 1856) was 16 miles from Perth; by now the rails had reached 400 feet and the summit soon followed. At Blackford (18 miles) the line passed through exposed country overlooked by moorland and ahead lay numerous heavy earthworks through glacial debris on the edge of Strathallan. The track then descended along the Allan Water valley to Stirling at gradients as steep as 1 in 74.

The Scottish Central made Perth its headquarters and established its workshops and main engine shed there. When the company was absorbed by the Caledonian on 5th July 1865 it was a very successful concern, operating 78 locomotives, nearly 300 carriages and over 1,300 wagons. No.123 pounded along Strathallan and Strathearn during the 'Races to Aberdeen' and passengers aboard the luxurious Aberdeen-Euston 'corridor expresses' enjoyed views of the Ochil Hills. Once again, an outline of the trains and motive power used on the former Scottish Central can be gleaned from earlier chapters.

Moncreiffe tunnel was used by all trains heading south from Perth, but after half a century it was causing serious concern. The fissured whinstone leaked water continuously and dampness, combined with sulphurous fumes from locomotives, was rotting the rock. Pieces regularly fell away, so every Sunday the bore was inspected and dangerous fragments removed. But the situation became so bad that a decision was taken to refurbish the tunnel and line it with brick. The process provides a fascinating insight into the scale of engineering work sometimes necessary to keep a main line railway running.

Work commenced in November 1901 and took until April 1904. It cost £42 a yard, as opposed to the £37 a yard required to create the tunnel in the first place. Firstly, the up line was removed and the down line slewed into the middle of the formation, making a single line block section worked from Friarton South and Hilton Junction signal boxes. Then a one foot gauge track was laid either side of the running line to carry a huge shield which followed the tunnel profile. Men worked above and behind the shield, protected from the 200 trains a day which still had to be accommodated. Fresh air was supplied from a compressor and electric lighting was installed.

Explosives were prohibited, so decayed rock had to be removed by drills and wedges, the work being mainly undertaken by Welsh and Cornish quarrymen on very high pay. At least six layers of brick were then put in place, although at one particularly bad spot the crown required no less than eleven feet of lining. Spoil removal was mainly done on Sundays when rail traffic was lighter. During the operation a huge timber building housing the compressor and concrete making plant was built on the side of the northern approach cutting. Grand new portals, exuding Edwardian confidence, were built at the conclusion of the work.

Local passenger services over the former Caledonian main line between Perth and Stirling ceased on 11th June 1956, resulting in the closure of seven stations, including Forgandenny, Forteviot, Dunning, Auchterarder and Blackford. Gleneagles remains open today. Goods facilities were withdrawn from Forgandenny on 28th October 1963, Dunning on 7th September 1964, Gleneagles on 2nd November 1964, Forteviot on 23rd May 1966 and Blackford on 11th September 1967. Auchterarder yard survived until 16th May 1983 after no less than seventeen years as an unstaffed public siding. In 1995 there were about twenty trains each way a day between Stirling and Perth, mainly class 158 diesel railcars from Glasgow to Aberdeen or Inverness and back.

D49 4-4-0 No 62725 INVERNESS-SHIRE at Blackford on 9th June 1956 with the very last up departure, the 7.06pm to Stirling, conveying just three passengers. The train had formed the 5.30pm from Glasgow Buchanan Street to Blackford, calling at all stations except Greenloaning, which had seen its last service earlier in the day.

GLENEAGLES TO CRIEFF

During the 1820s Crieff was considered important enough to warrant a

Birmingham/Sulzer type 2 No D5357 crosses the A9 at Blackford in charge of the 16.35 Dundee-Glasgow Queen Street on 25th March 1967. Blackford, a fairly substantial village, is off to the right but its station had been closed for over ten years. This bleak spot at the watershed of Strathearn and Strathallan is overlooked by 1,647 feet Wether Hill, whilst the cleft of Glen Eagles is in the distance. The A9 now crosses the railway by an overbridge on the Blackford bypass, although the level crossing remains for local traffic.

The curving, undulating, nature of the original Crieff branch was even apparent at the approach to Gleneagles. With Easter Greenwells farm and Muirtown Woods as a backdrop, Perth class 5 4-6-0 No 44998 slows for the junction station with an afternoon train from Crieff on 12th September 1963. A tender engine and two coaches provided the service when the railbus was not available - as was often the case!

waggonway from Aberdeen, as noted in an earlier chapter, but this never materialised. When the railway age proper began, this sedate and proud town of around four thousand inhabitants was left out in the cold, the proposed Scottish Central route passing eight miles to the south. So Crieff decided to build its own link to the national network, along the Pow valley. The Perth & Crieff District Railway was promoted in 1845 with landowners' support, the prospect of serving industry in the Almond valley as well as conveying Highland cattle being most encouraging. Unfortunately the Bill was rejected by Parliament because of Scottish Central opposition.

Overcoming their disappointment, the residents of Crieff decided to try again, this time for a branch from the main line near Auchterarder. The Crieff Junction Railway submission was successful and an Act was obtained on 15th August 1853. Thomas Bouch was appointed engineer because of his reputation for building such lines cheaply, and at a euphoric inaugural meeting he promised to complete the branch in less than a year for half the estimated cost. Wild optimism soon turned to frustration. The engineer never seemed to be available for consultation and by summer 1854 little work had been done.

Bouch eventually guaranteed to have the line ready by September 1855 and the somewhat naive directors took him at his word again. By that summer, staff had been recruited and items such as tickets and uniforms ordered. But as autumn approached there were still no stations, let along an operational railway. Employees drifted away and replacements were appointed; Muthill had three stationmasters before it even opened! Eventually the line was completed and the opening day was advertised as 13th March 1856. However, it appears that the Scottish Central refused to allow its trains on to the branch because of unsatisfactory points at Crieff Junction. Services began the following day, although the antics were far from over.

The local line seems to have had endless problems with its staff. When Crieff booking office was burgled, the stationmaster decided to have a change of career at short notice. One crossing keeper became so drunk that he kept a train waiting at the gates for some time before he could compose himself. A driver and guard refused to talk to each other following an argument and kept passengers amused for weeks. The Crieff Junction was taken over by the Scottish Central in 1865 and became Caledonian property within weeks. Under its new management the branch became an altogether more disciplined operation.

For most of its nine mile course the line descended into Strathearn from Crieff Junction, losing much of the altitude gained by the Scottish Central during its progress from Perth. There were seven overbridges and eight underbridges where the railway encountered roads and farm tracks, together with a dozen or so arches and culverts across minor tributaries of the Earn. A rather flimsy metal viaduct, later strengthened, crossed the river itself.

At Crieff Junction, the branch made a southwards-facing connection with the main line. It then turned north

On 4th July 1964 Park Royal railbus M79973 sways into Tullibardine, forming the 5.20pm from Crieff to Gleneagles. It was the last day of passenger services and although there were plenty of people on board enjoying a last trip on the branch, the decaying station was deserted. Considering it only served three or four farms this is hardly surprising.

and crossed the Perth-Dunblane road by a level crossing which was replaced by an underbridge on a deviation in 1919. Tullibardine station (just over 2 miles from Crieff Junction) stood at just below 300 feet and was a later addition. It was named after the surrounding estate, but served a few cottages and little else. A twisting descent with numerous cuttings and embankments followed, the train affording fine views of the wooded country leading down to Strathallan Castle (oddly enough in Strathearn). Muthill (5 miles) was around round 200 feet above sea level and two miles from the village. Only isolated farms kept it company. The rails were almost down to 100 feet where they crossed the River Earn, prior to the climb through Highlandman (7.5 miles) to Crieff at just less than 200 feet.

The Crieff branch had its own feeder line, about a mile of track conveying coal and other supplies to the famous Gleneagles Hotel. For many years the Caledonian nurtured an ambition to create the finest golfing centre in Britain, no doubt to outshine the other Scottish railway companies which served famous courses. Work began in late Edwardian times, Crieff Junction station being renamed Gleneagles on 1st April 1912 as a prelude. World War 1 interrupted progress, but the magnificent hotel was finally opened (by the LMS) in June 1924. It provided accommodation for up to 300 guests and boasted a ballroom with a stage, a grand corridor where the Gleneagles dance band performed, a swimming pool, postal and banking facilities, and 'wireless equipment by arrangement with the British Broadcasting Corporation'. Somewhat ominously, there was also a garage for a hundred motor cars and facilities for carrying out light repairs.

Gleneagles station had already been rebuilt in sumptuous style by the Caledonian during 1919. Previously, the original facilities, consisting of short platforms with ramshackle timber buildings, had sufficed. The sunken roadway approach, which usually became a quagmire in wet weather, was replaced by an elegant avenue flanked by trees and selected shrubs. Scottish baronial styling with crow-stepped gables and miniature turrets was adopted for the main building, and flower beds beautified the platforms and adjoining banks. There were even flowering plants in alcoves on the covered footbridge linking the platforms.

Unlike many rural towns in Tayside, Crieff prospered and grew, largely because the railway stimulated tourism. Large villas were built for summer visitors, Glenturret Distillery continued to produce its single malt, and the hydro remained popular. Later the town became a centre for china and glassware. A fairly frequent service was provided on the branch; in 1922 for example there were twelve trains from Gleneagles to Crieff, but by the early 1960s four-wheel railbuses were in use, a sure sign of a marginal line.

Passenger services between Gleneagles and Crieff were withdrawn on 6th July 1964, Tullibardine and Highlandman having been unstaffed halts since late 1959. Goods facilities fin-

Class 5 4-6-0 No 44705 crosses the bowstring spans of the River Earn viaduct, between Muthill and Highlandman, with the 4.35pm from Gleneagles to Crieff on 10th May 1958.

Highlandman station, looking south towards Muthill and Gleneagles on 25th August 1955. The little Crieff Junction Railway building is complemented by various items of railway furniture, including a derrick crane in the goods yard. The station, which was temporarily closed from 1st January 1916 to 1st February 1919, may have derived its name from the cattle drovers.

ished at Tullibardine on 2nd November 1959, but were still available at Muthill and Highlandman until 2nd November 1964. That meant the end of the branch, the section south of Muthill having already been abandoned on 1st September 1964. Crieff goods yard finally closed on 11th September 1967, the only access being from the Perth direction for the last three years. Gleneagles Hotel is as prestigious as ever, although it was privatised in 1984.

METHVEN AND COMRIE

Half a century after Crieff saw its first train, the town found itself on a coast to coast link between Dundee and Oban. However, this was certainly not a major trunk route; there were no through trains and two reversals would have been necessary anyway. The central section from Perth to Balquhidder was built in four stages by four different companies and proved to be a somewhat bucolic and pedestrian stretch of railway.

Methven is a small town some six miles west of Perth. It snuggles in the low hills between Glenalmond and the Pow Water valley, and has experienced troubled times. There were battles nearby in 1306 and 1644, whilst Margaret Tudor died in Methven Castle during 1541 after her husband James IV was killed at Flodden. In the less turbulent 1850s Methven's residents wanted a railway and decided to build it themselves. An Act for the Perth, Almond Valley and Methven Railway was acquired in 1856 and construction of the 6.5 mile branch from Almond Valley Junction on the Scottish North Eastern took just over a year.

Unfortunately the single track line displayed all the characteristics of a local promotion backed by limited funds, despite avoiding the irritating delays experienced by the Crieff Junction. A government inspector examined the track in October 1857 and discovered flimsy sand embankments in danger of slipping, a dearth of ballast and sleepers resting on bare clay in places. Two months later the inspector still described the branch as a possible danger to the public, but nevertheless allowed it to open. Traffic began on 1st January 1858.

From Almond Valley Junction, just under two miles north of Perth, the Methven branch curved west and ambled across the Almond meadows within sight of Huntingtower Castle, reaching 50 feet above sea level at Ruthven Road station (just over a mile from the junction). Almondbank station was a mile further on, and eventually branches served Lumsden & MacKenzie's bleach works (which had an overhead electric system) and a World War 2 Royal Naval Stores depot which was worked by a diesel shunter. Tibbermuir station (3.5 miles) stood at about 120 feet and was over half a mile from the hamlet of that name. This gentle progress continued past Mains of Tippermallo where the line curved northwards. But the last half mile from Burnside consisted of a fairly steep climb along a little wooded valley, at the top of which was Methven terminus, 200 feet up. Station buildings varied from a substantial house at Almondbank to a good imitation of a byre at Methven.

The branch was worked by the Scottish North Eastern at first, but in August 1858 the company bought a tank loco of its own. Shortly afterwards, four coaches it had hired from the main line company were also purchased, followed by another second-hand engine from the same source. The Perth-Methven service continued in its placid, parochial way until 28th October 1864 when the Almond Valley sold out to the Scottish North Eastern. It thus became a minor part of the Caledonian network less than two years later.

A private horse-drawn coach met the trains at Methven and provided a connection with Crieff during the summer months. Although there were insufficient passengers to justify a service for the rest of the year, this did not deter a local consortium from planning a railway to replace the coach. The Crieff & Methven Railway opened on 21st May 1866. It left the Methven branch a mile short of the terminus and pursued an easy course along the Pow Water Valley for over eleven miles, requiring just five overbridges and three underbridges, including one across

The driver of Wickham railbus SC79968 collects the single line token at Crieff, shortly after leaving on the 1.30pm run to Gleneagles on 2nd January 1960. Even this late, the generous trackwork representing the parallel Crieff Junction Railway and Crieff & Methven Railway approaches to the town, was still in situ.

the stream itself. Despite the lack of physical barriers, there were frequent changes in direction, resulting in fairly sharp curves.

A station purely for interchange purposes, boasting no less than three platforms, was provided at Methven Junction,. The line then headed west across Methven Moss before reaching remote Balgowan station (2.5 miles from the junction). Madderty station (5 miles) was named after a farm some distance away, although it stood next to the remains of Inchaffray Abbey. Gask Ridge rose to the south. This was a place of some significance in Roman times, and the remains of five signal stations together with the sites of five others are strung along a former military road. Abercairny station (7 miles) came next, followed by Innerpeffray (just over 9 miles), both of them serving isolated farms and little else. Thus far, the line had remained at 120-130 feet all the way from Methven Junction, but the last mile or so was on a rising gradient parallel to the Crieff Junction track.

The Crieff & Methven was worked by the Caledonian from the outset and absorbed by it in 1869. Although the stations had fairly substantial stone buildings, they never enjoyed a particularly generous passenger service, between four and six trains each way was the norm. Methven had eight services to Perth in the early years, but this was down to two in 1922. Nevertheless, the goods yards were important railheads for this agricultural district, particularly in the seed potato season.

Comrie, with a population of just over two thousand, joined the railway system on 1st June 1893 when the six mile Caledonian extension from Crieff opened. The town marks the beginning of the Highlands and is overlooked by the harsh crags of Crappich Hill (1,466 feet) and Mór Bheinn (2,100 feet). Despite the rugged nature of its surroundings, the line had a relatively easy passage alongside the River Earn. At first it clung to the northern bank, then there was a reverse curve through cuttings where the river cut through a ridge. The rest of the route lay across a broad flat stretch of valley floor between the mountains. At Crieff the old terminus was abandoned and a fine through station opened on the extension. Again the railway brought visitors and the town became a popular summer resort.

The final development was a link to Lochearnhead (which was renamed Balquhidder) on the Callander & Oban route, sanctioned in 1893. It was nominally built by the Comrie, St Fillans & Lochearnhead Railway, which was actually a Caledonian protégé. The line opened as far as St Fillans on 1st October 1901 and finally reached Balquhidder on 1st May 1905, encountering difficult terrain throughout. As far as St Fillans, it kept to the valley floor, crossing the River Earn four times to find a reasonable footing, but beyond here the track clung to the mountain side overlooking Loch Earn. It was a beautiful journey but passengers were scarce.

In summer 1922 eleven trains a day headed west from Crieff, three of them terminating at Comrie, another three going as far as St Fillans, and the remaining five continuing to Balquhidder. At the same time there were six trains between Perth and Crieff via Methven Junction. By the 1930s motor vehicles had eroded the already meagre traffic on some routes. The first passenger service to succumb was that to Methven, on 27th September 1937. A Sentinel steam car was used towards the end and those aboad often wondered whether they would reach the terminus as the carriage shuddered violently during the final climb, its wheels sinking into every joint.

World War 2 only delayed the inevitable, passenger services from Perth to Crieff via Methven Junction and Comrie to Balquhidder being withdrawn on 1st October 1951. Innerpeffray and the line

As the worst of the winter passed into memory, traces of snow lingered at Crieff on 12th March 1955. Class 5 4-6-0 No 45016 waited in the substantial and attractive station with the 12.07pm to Gleneagles. The elegant stone houses of Crieff climb up the lower slopes of Knock of Crieff to form a fine backdrop.

beyond Comrie closed completely at the same time. Goods traffic ceased at Tibbermuir on 27th January 1964 and Comrie on 15th June 1964, the latter losing its passenger trains three weeks later when the Gleneagles-Crieff-Comrie service finished. Monday 25th January 1965 was another bad day - the yards at Almondbank and Madderty closed, parcels were no longer accepted at Methven Junction (there was no goods yard here) and the Methven branch became redundant. Perth to Crieff followed on 11th September 1967 with the closure of Crieff and Balgowan yards, access having been by way of Perth New Yard rather than Almond Valley Junction since 1962.

Crieff train services, Monday to Saturday, Summer 1948
SO - Saturdays only
SX - Saturdays excepted

Gleneagles to Crieff
6.40am (to Balquhidder)
8.40am
11.20am (to Comrie)
3.00pm (to St Fillans)
5.25pm
6.20pm (through coaches from Edinburgh Princes Street)
7.35pm (to Comrie SX on request)
8.55pm SO

Crieff to Gleneagles
8.08am (through coaches St Fillans to Edinburgh Princes Street)
10.05am (ex Balquhidder)
12.12pm
2.25pm
3.40pm
5.25pm (ex St Fillans)
7.00pm
8.28pm SO
Also:
12.10pm Comrie to Crieff
2.25pm Balquhidder to Crieff
7.40pm SX Balquhidder to Crieff

Perth to Crieff
10.00am
12.30pm (to Balquhidder)
4.17pm
5.22pm (to Balquhidder)

Crieff to Perth
8.05am
10.18am
1.52pm SO
6.05pm
8.45pm SO (ex Balquhidder, non stop Crieff to Perth)

Fowler 4F 0-6-0 No 44193 at Crieff with the 5.24pm to Gleneagles on 25th August 1955. Details of the 1893 Caledonian architecture are well shown in this view, notably the forest of shapely little chimneys and the grand columns with highly decorative capitals supporting the canopy. No trace of the station remains today.

Pickersgill 4-4-0 No 54500 poses outside the twin loco sheds at Crieff on 16th July 1956. These were built by the Crieff Junction and Crieff & Methven companies respectively, but proved too small for most passenger engines in later years. At one time there had been yet a third shed at Crieff.

Despite the generous provision of three platform faces, Methven Junction station was incredibly remote, the only access being a mile long track from Methven itself. This passed through the yard of Mains of Tippermallo farm and came in behind the cattle dock on the right. Ex-Caledonian 4-2-2 No 123 paused at Methven Junction with a special on 11th October 1958.

Above. **Closed Innerpeffray station, once owned by the Crieff & Methven Railway, looking towards Methven Junction on 10th May 1958. The neat and sizeable stone building stood in open fields a couple of miles east of Crieff. It had to compete with nearby Highlandman on the Gleneagles line for the sparse traffic on offer, and also closed on 1st January 1916, as a temporary wartime economy measure.**

Below. **Comrie station on 25th August 1955, briefly brought to life by the only arrival of the day at that time. Ex-LMS 4F 0-6-0 No 44193 had just arrived with a through coach off the 4.25pm from Edinburgh Princes Street to Crieff. Pleasant timber buildings with ornate canopy dripboards enhanced this Caledonian station.**

Above. **Ex-Caledonian 0-4-4T No.55209 (which had acquired a chimney off a former North British N15 0-6-2T) at Ladybank with the 4.00pm from Perth on 19th April 1954. The train was twenty minutes late leaving Perth because it waited for two passengers on a late running Inverness - Glasgow service. That brought the total aboard the local to six! Note Ladybank shed in the distance and the rather unassuming station building.**

Below. **Preserved North British 4-4-0 No.256 GLEN DOUGLAS at Newburgh on 17th June 1960 with the RCTS/SLS 'Scottish Tour' which comprised a motley collection of restored Caledonian, ex-LNER and BR Standard coaches, including a cafeteria car. B1 4-6-0 No.61330 is shunting the goods yard.**

CHAPTER 8

PERTH - SOUTHERN APPROACHES

Of all the railway approaches to Perth, that from the south saw the most proposals, and inevitably the greatest number of shattered dreams. That was back in the 1840s, when the race was on to create a route from Edinburgh to Perth and Dundee, although the Glasgow - Dundee corridor also generated interest. Topography was an important consideration, the Ochil Hills forming a formidable barrier south of the Tay and the Lomond and Cleish Hills rising abruptly from the plain around Loch Leven. There were also local economic factors, notably the highly productive Fife coalfield and the growing industrial area around Alloa, also based on coal. During the late 1850s the little town of Kinross received more than its fair share of attention from railway promoters.

At first, the outcome of all this speculation was a Y-shaped main line across the middle of Fife. The Edinburgh & Northern was a prosperous if strange creature, with two of its limbs terminating at ferries across the Forth and Tay estuaries respectively, and a third joining the Scottish Central two miles short of Perth. This latter arrangement caused all manner of acrimony for some years. Then came three parochial branches, converging on Kinross from the north east, south and west, all of them initially owned by local companies with limited resources. During 1890 two of these minor lines had greatness thrust upon them when they became part of a fast route between Edinburgh and Perth via the Forth Bridge. A new line through the Ochils at Glen Farg opened at the same time. Ironically, only the old Edinburgh & Northern route survives today.

EDINBURGH & NORTHERN

Ideas for a line between the Forth and Tay, tapping the Fife coalfield, were first aired in 1840. Engineer John Milne proposed the Western Fife Railway which would head north west from Kirkcaldy, skirt Loch Leven and reach the shore at Newburgh where a somewhat adventurous bridge would take the tracks into Perthshire. An alternative project was the Eastern Fife Railway, championed by Thomas Grainger. The plan was to run a line from Burntisland to Ferryport-on-Craig (later Tayport) via Cupar, ferries meeting the trains at either end. Neither progressed beyond the discussion stage, but over the next five years Fife was never out of the limelight. In 1843 the Perth & Fife Railway actually made it to Westminster, although the proposal was rejected by the House of Commons because of insufficient planning. With the 'mania' in full flush, this was resurrected as the Edinburgh & Northern and this time success beckoned despite a bewildering plethora of other submissions.

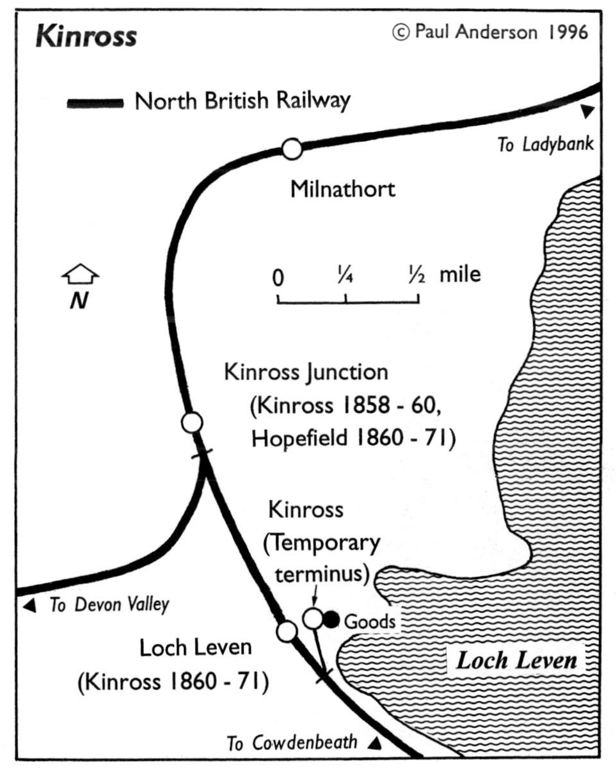

The Edinburgh & Northern Railway received its Act on 31st July 1845, in the face of no less than sixteen rival schemes. These included the Edinburgh & Perth and Scottish South Midland Junction, both of which are outlined later. From Burntisland the new line was to head for Ladybank and Newburgh before bridging the Tay to join the Dundee & Perth. A branch from Ladybank to Cupar was also authorised. Connections to and from Edinburgh would be provided by the Granton - Burntisland ferry and the Edinburgh, Leith & Granton Railway. However, all manner of modifications, deviations and additions were needed before the line assumed its final form.

Perth harbour trustees belatedly raised strong objections to the proposed bridge on the grounds that it would hinder navigation. Fortunately, the Edinburgh & Northern saw an easy way of avoiding a conflict. A local company, the Strathearn Railway, had already gained approval for a link between Newburgh and the Scottish Central at Hilton, immediately south of Moncreiffe tunnel. By an Act of 3rd July 1846 the larger concern acquired these powers and abandoned the estuary crossing. This solved the immediate difficulties but stored up problems for the future. The same Act approved an extension from Cupar to Ferryport-on-Craig and various branches.

Progress was rapid on the 67 miles of track. Eighteen separate contracts were let, virtually all to local firms who knew the ground well, and work on them proceeded concurrently. Over 7,000 men were employed at one stage. The company expected a lot of business from the Fife coalfield and ordered an astonishing 600 wagons - it proved a wise decision. With completion imminent, the Edinburgh & Northern absorbed the Edinburgh, Leith & Granton on 22nd July 1847, thus ensuring an independent route to the heart of the capital.

There was much rejoicing on 20th September 1847 when the line to Perth opened as far as a temporary station at Abdie, just over two miles east of Newburgh. The branch from Ladybank to Cupar opened at the same time and this

Ex-LMS Compound 4-4-0 No.40939 stands at Newburgh with the 4.10pm from Perth to Ladybank on 23rd May 1955 - the crew enjoying a leisurely chat while station staff load rolls of floorcloth from a local factory. The passenger service was withdrawn four months later.

reached Ferryport-on-Craig (see Chapter 9). Completion of the Perth route was in stages. An extension of a mile or so took the track to a second temporary platform called Glenbirnie on 9th December 1847. The line proceeded to a third makeshift station at Abernethy Road on 17th May 1848 and a connection at Hilton Junction was made on 18th July 1848.

From Burntisland the Edinburgh & Northern followed the Firth of Forth coast through Kirkcaldy before veering away northwards towards Thornton and Markinch (13 miles from Burntisland). After a viaduct over the River Ore just south of Markinch the track climbed from 170 feet to over 300 feet at Kirkforthar. Falkland Road station (16 miles) was just beyond the summit. Falkland itself, an ancient Royal Burgh with cobbled streets and a fine Renaissance palace, stood below the Lomond Hills two miles to the west. Between Kingskettle (18 miles) and Ladybank (18.75 miles) the line dipped to 140 feet where it bridged the River Eden. The climb out of the Howe of Fife through Edensmuir Forest led to Collessie (21.5 miles).

Ahead, the eastern flanks of the Ochils only reached 600-700 feet here, but nevertheless formed a significant obstacle. Fortunately there was a way through. The railway first curved westwards through Collessie Den alongside a stream draining Black Loch, then turned northwards and squeezed between two hills overlooking Lindores Loch. From a 260ft summit, it was downhill through cuttings until a fine prospect of the Tay estuary opened up. Beyond the harbour town of Newburgh (26.5 miles) the track kept to the lower slopes of Pitcairlie Hill as far as Abernethy (29 miles), then crossed the flood plain of the River Earn. After Bridge of Earn (33 miles) a sweeping curve took the track over the river and on to Hilton Junction (34.5 miles).

The first passenger services consisted of four trains each way between Burntisland and Cupar, coaches providing connections to and from Dundee via the ferry. Loadings were well above predictions and the new railway was the subject of glowing reports in the press. Mineral traffic also grew rapidly as south west Fife became industrialised. In fact the area eventually produced over nine million tons of coal a year, virtually all of it carried by the North British which had inherited the Hilton Junction - Burntisland line and its branches. The railway also stimulated the local floorcloth industry which emerged from the manufacture of canvas sails and evolved into linoleum production. On 1st April 1849 the Edinburgh & Northern changed its name to the more descriptive Edinburgh, Perth & Dundee Railway.

Despite this early success, there were infuriating disputes over the approach to Perth. The Scottish Central and Edinburgh & Northern operated competing services between Perth and Edinburgh, but they managed to agree a rate for running powers over the two miles north of Hilton Junction. Eighteen months later the agreement collapsed when the Edinburgh, Perth & Dundee innocently signed a deal with the Forth & Clyde Canal for the transhipment of coal traffic. A succession of flimsy contracts were implemented, amended and abandoned, then a bout of fare cutting raged. The Scottish Central also charged tolls for the use of Moncreiffe tunnel and decided to raise these without warning, despite the six months notice required. Trains were halted at Hilton Junction and passengers in Caledonian, Edinburgh & Glasgow and Edinburgh, Perth & Dundee carriages had to pay up. Timekeeping became chaotic, so after much haggling a system of annual payments was agreed. Income amounted to no less than £8,000 a year.

With this irritation out of the way, the Edinburgh, Perth & Dundee settled down and flourished as the main route

The original Bridge of Earn station was beyond the road overbridge in the left background of this view, but on 1st February 1892 new facilities in the simplest North British style were provided, so that trains using the Glen Farg line could call. On 28th May 1960 A2 Pacific No.60530 SAYAJIRAO passes through with the 4.03pm from Edinburgh Waverley to Perth and Inverness. The Glenfarg tracks curve away to the right behind the footbridge.

No tolls to pay at Hilton Junction on 27th April 1963. Gresley A4 Pacific No.60012 COMMONWEALTH OF AUSTRALIA about to join the former Scottish Central line south of Perth with the 10.03am from Edinburgh Waverley to Perth via Glenfarg. The ever-present Ochil Hills form the skyline.

from Edinburgh to the north. The company remained independent until absorbed by the North British on 1st August 1862. When the Forth Bridge and its associated works were completed in 1890, most of the Burntisland - Perth line became busier than ever. However, the section between Ladybank and Bridge of Earn was reduced to a secondary route - it was singled by the LNER and lost its passenger services in the mid-1950s (see later) but managed to survive as a freight line. In the mid-1970s it became part of the main Edinburgh - Perth route once again.

KINROSS

The most famous asset of Kinross is undoubtedly Loch Leven. This large natural lake, two miles wide and four miles long, contains two islands. One of them has the remains of St. Serf's Priory, whilst the other is dominated by a ruined castle where Mary Queen of Scots was imprisoned. Fishermen throughout the world know the loch for its pink-fleshed trout, and it has long been a popular venue for skating and curling when frozen. The Lomond Hills rear up to the east, Benarty Hill and the Cleish Hills form the southern skyline, and rising ground away to the north and west heralds the Ochil Hills, together creating a beautiful setting.

Kinross itself is a small market town with a population of around 2,500 but it has always been the centre of a productive agricultural area and even in 1850 there were some two thousand residents. By that time the Scottish Central had been built beyond the Ochils away to the north west, and the Edinburgh, Perth & Dundee passed nearly twelve miles to the east. The abortive Edinburgh & Perth had promised Kinross a branch, but the town had to be content with a horse bus connection from Falkland Road. In the mid to late 1850s there came a flurry of railway promotion locally, involving lines from Ladybank, Cowdenbeath and Tillicoultry near Alloa, all focusing on Kinross.

The Fife & Kinross intended to provide a direct link with the Edinburgh - Perth main line. Its Act of 16th July 1855 authorised the section from Ladybank to Milnathort, and the short extension to Kinross was approved on 10th August 1857. Following the sod-cutting ceremony at Auchtermuchty on 14th January 1856 work proceeded rapidly, for there were no problems with either land purchase or engineering work. The branch reached Strathmiglo on 6th June 1857, Milnathort on 9th March 1858 and Kinross on 20th August 1858.

Curving away from the main line at Ladybank, the single track Fife & Kinross headed west across the almost level Howe of Fife, maintaining an altitude of about 130 feet with long straights and sudden curves. The small market town of Auchtermuchty was reached after four and a quarter miles, and the station was just to the south near Myres Castle. By now, high ground was beginning to close in, the Ochils stretching away to the north with the twin peaks of East Lomond (1,394 feet) and West Lomond (1,713 feet) rising abruptly to the south. A stiff climb up the headwaters of the River Eden followed. From 150 feet just beyond Auchtermuchty, the branch reached 200 feet at Strathmiglo (6.25 miles) before pursuing a wriggling course, crossing the Eden no less than seven times. Gateside station (8.25 miles) stood at 250 feet, the track topped 300 feet at Bennety Mill, Burnside Farm was passed at 350 feet and Mawcarse station (11 miles) was close to 400 feet. The line stayed at this level for the run to Milnathort (13.5 miles) and the sweeping curve to Kinross (14.75 miles).

Fife & Kinross directors asked the Edinburgh, Perth & Dundee to work their line, but the larger company insisted it could not spare any engines. So three 0-4-0 tender locos were purchased from Hawthorn of Leith, and rolling stock ordered from a local blacksmith. Maybe as a result of dubious craftsmanship - or, more likely, indifferent maintenance - two of the coaches were described as 'partly rotten' by 1861. Even worse, the company never had enough wagons and at busy periods discovered that all its stock was elsewhere in Scotland!

The Kinross-shire Railway acquired its Act of Parliament on 10th August 1857. At just seven miles, it was only half the length of the Kinross & Fife, yet construction was prolonged and the line did not open until 20th June 1860. It began at Lumphinnans near Cowdenbeath on the Thornton - Dunfermline route, which had been authorised by the 1846 Edinburgh & Northern Act and opened in

Auchtermuchty station, closed to passengers in 1950, was visited by the RCTS/SLS 'Scottish Tour' on 17th June 1960. Preserved North British 4-4-0 No.256 GLEN DOUGLAS was in charge of the train. At the time, stored coaches and wagons occupied a stub of the line to Ladybank, through workings having ceased in 1957. The Fife & Kinross station building, solidly built of stone, was attached to the goods shed, an eccentric practice not uncommon on locally promoted lines.

1848-49. It headed more or less north westwards, twisting and turning to take account of the contours of Blairadam Forest, Benarty Hill and the Cleish uplands. The branch both started and finished around the 400 feet mark, but in between it was a series of minor switchbacks determined by the eastward - draining Lochfitty Burn, River Ore, Gairney Water and Bog Burn. Colliery subsidence eventually made the undulations even worse. Intermediate stations were at Kelty (serving the nearby colliery village) and remote Blairadam, named after a large house over a mile away.

By 1860 the Edinburgh, Perth & Dundee motive power situation had clearly improved, the company agreeing to work the Kinross-shire - providing the latter bought an engine as well. This materialised as a Hawthorn 0-4-0, similar to those on the Fife & Kinross. For three months, the branch from Lumphinnans operated as a somewhat peripheral appendix of Fife's railway system. Its approach to Kinross along the attractive western shore of Loch Leven led to a terminus on the southern outskirts of the town, but this was only a temporary measure. A one mile extension of the Fife & Kinross had been authorised on 28th June 1858, the connection opening for goods on 20th September 1860, and passengers shortly afterwards. It incorporated a new joint station (bearing the name Kinross) just north of the temporary Kinross-shire terminus, with the former Fife & Kinross terminus renamed Hopefield in December 1860.

The two small companies, serving agricultural and farming districts respectively, got on remarkably well. Each of them ran two return services a day which connected at Kinross, and they apportioned long distance bookings on a fair basis. Independence was short-lived however, the Kinross-shire selling out to the Edinburgh, Perth & Dundee on 1st August 1861, followed by the Fife & Kinross on 29th July 1862. A couple of days later, both branches became part of the North British Railway. Under this new management, the impact of the railway on the local economy became clearer. For instance, the linen industry at Auchtermuchty flourished as it reached new markets, whilst the manufacture of shawls and plaids at Kinross faded away when it lost its local monopoly.

A third route headed for Kinross from the west. The Devon Valley Railway was less than fourteen miles long, yet no less than sixteen years elapsed between promotion and completion. In fact, on the opening day the contractor exclaimed that he had never known a project so beset with troubles. Although the Devon Valley was a highly scenic local line, constantly in the shadow of the Ochils, it was a manifestation of greater ambitions and carried through trains from Glasgow to Perth for most of its existence.

The Scottish South Midland Junction, one of the many mania schemes involving Fife, aimed to provide a direct link from Clydeside to Tayside via the Devon Valley and a bridge at Newburgh, but it failed to make progress. Nevertheless the Alloa area was becoming increasingly industrialised and a line to Dunfermline was completed in 1850, followed by the westwards extension to Stirling in 1852. Meanwhile, a branch from Alloa to the manufacturing town of Tillicoultry opened on 3rd June 1851. A connection from there to the Edinburgh, Perth & Dundee seemed an attractive proposition as it would create a secondary route from Glasgow to Dundee.

In September 1855 a meeting was held to assess support for the proposed Devon Valley Railway. By this time the Fife & Kinross had been authorised so it was only necessary to consider a link between Tillicoultry and Kinross. Unfortunately there was little enthusiasm locally but eventually both the Edinburgh & Glasgow and Scottish Central agreed to subscribe substantial sums, the latter seeing the new line as a way of reaching the Fife coalfield. The Devon Valley received its Act of Parliament on 23rd August 1858, an occasion overshadowed by the withdrawal of financial backing from the two larger companies three weeks earlier.

Cash was in short supply, although the Fife & Kinross was very supportive and helped to raise funds. The sod-cutting ceremony took place on 4th August 1860 but actual construction work had to wait until further capital had been accumulated. Maybe because of their gratitude to the Fife & Kinross, the Devon Valley directors decided to build westwards from Kinross until money ran out. It was favourable terrain and the line opened to Crook of Devon and Rumbling Bridge on 1st August 1863. Ahead lay the Devon gorge where the river dropped 400 feet in less than five miles - a daunting prospect for railway construction. Instead, the company opted for the other easy section, from Tillicoultry to Dollar, brought into use on 3rd May 1869.

Salvation came in 1866 when the expansionist North British realised that a link from Alloa to Kinross would be a useful asset, enabling it to compete with the Caledonian for Glasgow - Perth traffic. With this new source of cash and engineering expertise, the Devon Valley became reality. Taking the existing line on from Rumbling Bridge would have demanded gradients as steep as 1 in 50, so the section west of Crook of Devon was closed from 1st October 1868 to 1st October 1870 for realignment. Even so, stretches of 1 in 63 and 1 in 70 were necessary. Two viaducts, seventeen bridges and a host of earthworks were also required. The Devon Valley railway finally opened as a through route on 1st May 1871 and to avoid confusion Hopefield was renamed Kinross Junction on 16th October, Kinross becoming Loch Leven at the same time.

A journey from Kinross Junction to Tillicoultry revealed the three construction phases. After curving away from the Ladybank - Cowdenbeath line, the branch headed west along the broad Gelly Burn Valley with the Ochils and Cleish Hills well to the north and south respectively. Cleish Road station (two miles from Kinross Junction) served a scattering of farms and was named after a hamlet over two miles distant. It became Balado in June 1878, the inspiration this time being an isolated country house. The line climbed slightly from 400 feet at Kinross to 450 feet by Crook of Devon (5.25 miles). This village was named after the 180 degree turn which the river made nearby, during its strange course from the Ochils high above Alloa to the River Forth just west of the same town.

The realigned section to Rumbling Bridge (6.75 miles) brought the track down to 400 feet again, then the descent began in earnest. A curve, partly on embankments, led to Gairney Glen viaduct at 350 feet. This five-arch structure, 360 feet long and 110 feet high, overlooked a wooded ravine culminating in a waterfall. A hillside course with occasional views of the Devon gorge and numerous earthworks, including a slip-prone cutting through glacial sand at Arndean, took the rails to the 250 feet contour at Blairingone. Devon viaduct, an elegant curved structure 390 feet long, 52 feet high and formed of six arches, carried the line across the river. Half a mile of embankment led to Dollar, 11 miles from Kinross Junction and 100 feet above sea level. A gentle descent to Tillicoultry (13.75 miles) was over relatively easy ground between the meandering Devon and the steep Ochil ramparts.

North British locos and stock worked the Devon Valley from the outset, and it was absorbed by the larger company in July 1875. At first the line carried what was basically a local service linking Ladybank and Kinross with Alloa and Stirling, passengers between Perth and Glasgow preferring the much shorter Caledonian route. For a brief period there were through carriages from Glasgow to Dundee and Aberdeen via Kinross, following completion of the first Tay Bridge. With the opening of the Bridge of Earn - Mawcarse line in 1890, services between Perth and Glasgow became viable, the North British putting on five each way over the Devon Valley route and a similar number via the Forth Bridge. By then, the scenic nature of the line through Rumbling Bridge and Dollar was seen as a selling point and it was designated the 'picturesque route'.

GLENFARG

The Ochil Hills are largely made up of inhospitable moorland culminating in scores of summits ranging from 2,363 feet Ben Clach north of Alloa to 923 feet Pitcairlie Hill behind Newburgh. There are two significant passes, both of which received attention from railway mania schemes. A Scottish South Midland Junction branch would have run from Rumbling Bridge to Auchterarder via Glen Devon and Glen Eagles, but the whole ambitious project

Fairburn 2-6-4T No.42693 at Dollar with the 2.28pm from Stirling on 11th April 1959. King's Seat Hill (2,111 feet) in the background dominates the small Devon Valley town. Further west at Tillicoultry, the Ochils rise even more precipitously, from 50 to 1,500 feet in just over a quarter of a mile.

came to nought, as noted earlier. The Edinburgh & Perth actually received North British cash for its line through Glen Farg until the latter's Lancashire backers found out and insisted that aid was withdrawn, thus effectively killing off the Fife project. For 45 years the Ochils remained undisturbed by locomotives, the routes from Glasgow and Edinburgh to Perth skirting the defiant volcanic slopes.

As the nineteenth century entered its last two decades, railways became supremely self-confident and one of the greatest manifestations of this was the Forth Bridge. It gave the East Coast route a distinctive edge over the West Coast consortium for Dundee and Aberdeen traffic, and played its part in the 1895 races (see Chapter 4). Business from the Highlands and Perth was also seen as fair game by the North British, although several improvements were necessary to capture it.

A new line from Inverkeithing near the northern end of the bridge to the ferry terminal at Burntisland connected with former Edinburgh & Northern tracks, but the route to Perth via Ladybank and Newburgh was unacceptably roundabout. As a result, an existing line from Inverkeithing to Dunfermline was improved, a cut-off built at Cowdenbeath and the old Kinross-shire and Fife & Kinross formation from Kelty to Mawcarse was upgraded and doubled, achieving a status which the local promoters could hardly have envisaged. Ahead lay the Ochil barrier, conveniently breached where the River Farg had carved a deep valley on its way down to the Tay estuary. Bridge of Earn was just eight miles away from Mawcarse in a straight line, and a short cut between them was clearly justified despite the heavy capital expenditure involved. An Act of 3rd July 1882 sanctioned the new railway, together with the improvements mentioned above.

From just below 400 feet at Mawcarse, the line headed north then north west, climbing gently with the River Eden headwaters for company. It reached the summit around 470 feet in a cutting near the village of Glenfarg, over three miles from Mawcarse. The juvenile River Farg appeared from the west, having drained the slopes of Tillyrie, Golloch and Deuglie, and six miles of descent at gradients as steep as 1 in 74 commenced. For three miles the track negotiated a deep, thickly wooded defile. Numerous rock cuttings were required and both the river and parallel road had to be diverted in places. At Meikle Fildie the line dropped below 400 feet again.

Suddenly the river turned eastwards, looping past Bein Inn, but the railway carried straight on. A viaduct spanned the Farg, then the tracks immediately plunged into a 507 yard tunnel through the intervening spur (5.5 miles). By now the line was down to 300 feet, the descent continuing through woodland below Pottiehill. A problem of a different sort lay ahead. The Ochils ended in a steep slope of several hundred feet overlooking eastern Strathearn, but the railway had to lose height gradually. A sweeping ninety degree curve took the formation out of the Farg valley, through a 517 yard tunnel (6.5 miles) and obliquely down the side of Balmanno Hill. At 200 feet the line abandoned the Ochils, pushed north across the carselands past the hamlet of Dron, and completed its long descent at Bridge of Earn, less than 50 feet above sea level and ten miles from Mawcarse.

Class 5 4-6-0 No.44908 running into Glenfarg on 28th May 1960, with the 4.30pm Glasgow Queen Street to Perth via the Devon Valley. Although it merely served a village on the southern slopes of the Ochils, the only intermediate station on the Mawcarse - Bridge of Earn line had a rather fine stone building with hipped and gabled roofs, big chimneys and a sizeable platform canopy.

Goods traffic began to use the Glanfarg route on 15th May 1890 and passenger services between Edinburgh Waverley and Perth via the Forth Bridge commenced on 2nd June 1890. Expresses made their way through the Ochils for nearly eighty years and for much of that time the basic pattern of services remained the same. In summer 1957 for example, there were nine northbound and eight southbound trains, taking 1 hours 31 minutes to 1 hour 39 minutes for the 48 miles between Edinburgh and Perth. This included four or five intermediate stops and took account of subsidence slacks in the Fife coalfield. An improvement came with the 'Fair Maid' introduced that September, the northbound service taking 1 hour 28 minutes with just one stop at Dunfermline.

By 1957 the North British Atlantics and 4-4-0s were just a memory in Glen Farg and Class 5 4-6-0s, B1 4-6-0s, V2 2-6-2s and LNER Pacifics were the norm. Diesels were on the way and they led to a further acceleration in services; in September 1968 the 09.45 Edinburgh - Perth took just 1 hour 7 minutes to reach Perth. Less than eighteen months later there were no trains at all and the M90 motorway soon obliterated most of the former trackbed. The Glenfarg closure came at the end of half a century of retrenchment which almost resulted in the complete demise of Perth's southern approaches.

Loch Leven lost its passenger trains on 1st November 1921, followed by Blairadam on 22nd September 1930, and most of the Ladybank - Bridge of Earn line was singled in 1933. Ladybank - Kinross passenger services ceased on 5th June 1950, involving the closure of Auchtermuchty, Strathmiglo and Gateside stations and Ladybank - Perth trains finished on 19th September 1955, with the loss of Collessie, Newburgh and Abernethy stations. Falkland Road saw its last passengers on 15th September 1958.

As road transport became dominant, goods yards were gradually abandoned: Abernethy on 16th August 1956; Kingskettle on 2nd May 1960; Collessie on 1st March 1962. The Beeching report finished off most of the rest: Blairadam on 23rd March 1964; Balado, Crook of Devon and Rumbling Bridge on 20th April 1964; Falkland Road on 10th August 1964; Auchtermuchty, Strathmiglo and Gateside on 5th October 1964. The last closure meant the end of the old Fife & Kinross line east of Mawcarse, apart from private sidings at Gateside. Meanwhile, Perth - Stirling passenger trains via the Devon Valley ceased on 15th June 1964, resulting in the demise of stations at Bridge of Earn, Glenfarg, Mawcarse, Milnathort, Balado, Crook of Devon, Rumbling Bridge, Dollar and Tillicoultry. The Kinross - Tillicoultry section closed completely at the same time.

Mawcarse yard finished on 25th January 1965 followed by Loch Leven (the depot for Kinross) on 29th March 1965, and Glenfarg and Bridge of Earn on 21st June 1965. Kingskettle lost its passenger trains on 4th September 1967, but far more serious was the withdrawal of Edinburgh - Perth expresses via Cowdenbeath, Kinross Junction and Glenfarg on 5th January 1970. The line south of Milnathort was retained for seed potato traffic until 4th May 1970. For nearly six years there were no passenger trains at all on the southern approaches until the Ladybank - Hilton Junction line began to carry Edinburgh - Perth services again on 6th October 1975. In 1995 there were six northbound and five southbound trains over the route, 1 hour 13 minutes being the best time between the two cities.

***Top.* Confident engineering work was characteristic of the Glenfarg line. V2 2-6-2 No.60931 drifts down the face of Balmanno Hill at the head of a northbound freight on 10th August 1963, the Ochils receding away in a humid haze.**

***Middle.* Birmingham/Sulzer type 2 diesels Nos D5343 and D5344, two miles into the climb from Bridge of Earn to Glenfarg on 10th August 1963 with the 3.15pm from Perth to Edinburgh Waverley, which included through coaches from both Inverness and Nairn. Balmanno signal cabin (closed as long ago as 1926) is on the left, whilst the hamlet of Dron and Balmanno Castle are hidden by the trees on the right.**

***Left.* Standard Class 5 4-6-0 No.73107 on the approach to Balmanno, storming up the first part of the climb to Glenfarg with a southbound freight on 10th August 1963. Moncreiffe Hill is prominent on the skyline.**

An unidentified J37 0-6-0 crosses the Tay Bridge with a couple of dozen empties, probably returning to the Fife coalfield, on 17th November 1962. The forlorn stumps are a lasting memorial to Bouch's ill-fated bridge and a strong easterly wind snatches smoke from the engine - just as it did on that disastrous night 83 years previously.

Chapter 9

CROSSING THE TAY

Despite the intervening expanse of water where the River Tay swells out to join the sea, northern Fife has long been dominated by Dundee. For centuries, sailing craft plied across the estuary from Newport and Ferryport-on-Craig. Then came the railway ferries with track incorporated in their decks, a brainwave of Thomas Bouch which established his reputation as an innovative engineer. Thirty years later the same man was responsible for the first Tay Bridge, another bold venture - but one which failed disastrously and ended his career. For the past two decades the Tay Road Bridge has provided the main link between Fife and the former county of Angus.

From Ladybank the River Eden flows north eastwards along a broad valley towards St Andrews Bay, and the Edinburgh & Northern route through Cupar followed Stratheden as far as Leuchars. From here the line headed north across the bleak expanse of Tent's Muir to Ferryport-on-Craig. Leuchars was also the junction for an early branch from historic St Andrews. East of Newburgh the Ochils make their last defiant stand. The line from Leuchars to the Tay Bridge negotiated the eastern extremity of the uplands past St Fort, whilst a very late branch from Newburgh to St Fort wriggled through the hills.

Inevitably the Tay Bridge itself dominates this final section of the book, and it neatly brings us back to Dundee where the story of Tayside's railways began in Chapter 1. The construction, collapse and subsequent rebuilding of the great viaduct have been well chronicled elsewhere, but an outline is clearly essential here. However, the busy commuter line through Newport, prompted and sustained by the bridge, is not forgotten.

LEUCHARS CHURCH

TAYPORT

Fife has always been proudly independent and flourished well before railways arrived. Its prosperity, particularly in the north, was largely based on agriculture. Very fertile soil, together with enlightened landowners who established specially planned farming villages, meant that there was a surplus of produce for export to other areas of Scotland. Cupar, with a population of around 4,500 by the end of the 18th century, was an important centre for this trade. The town was also a stopping point for the Edinburgh-Arbroath stagecoaches, but these took up to two days for the journey because of rough roads and two ferry crossings. Express mails to Aberdeen actually took less time, although these travelled via Perth and prestigious coaches such as the 'Strathmore Diligence' were hauled by four horses.

Robert Stevenson aired the idea of a waggonway from Edinburgh to Dundee in 1819 and the potentially rich pickings of Fife gave rise to the first serious railway proposals two decades later. The Edinburgh & Northern of 1845 was originally conceived as a line from Burntisland to Perth with a spur to Cupar, as discussed in Chapter 8. However, the rival Edinburgh & Perth scheme included a branch

Vintage paddle steamer B L NAIRN arrives at Newport with four or five cars and a few foot passengers on 3rd January 1959. Freighters berthed outside Dundee docks can be seen above the pier.

Diesel ferry ABERCRAIG leaving Dundee for Newport on 28th August 1954. This long established crossing was almost made redundant by the Tay Bridge, but was saved by the emergence of motor vehicles and survived until the Tay Road Bridge opened.

to the seaward end of the Tay estuary and forced the Edinburgh & Northern to think again. The planned extension from Cupar was to culminate in a two mile bridge across the water to the centre of Dundee, but vehement protests from the Admiralty and Perth Harbour led to the revised route to Ferryport-on-Craig, authorised on 3rd July 1846. In anticipation of parliamentary approval, the Edinburgh & Northern purchased the ferry in February of that year. On 22nd July 1847 the company acquired an Act to rebuild the harbour, despite objections from Dundee seamen, and the name Tayport was adopted.

The Ladybank-Cupar section opened on 20th September 1847, with remarkably popular coach connections to Dundee. Services were extended to Tayport on 17th May 1848. At Ladybank the branch veered eastwards from the Perth line and initially ran across the eastern part of the Howe of Fife. This more or less level section, at around 130 feet above sea level, continued as far as Springfield (three miles from Ladybank) where Stratheden proper began. High ground pinched the valley and the line was overlooked by Walton Hill and Hill of Tarvit for the run to Cupar (5.5 miles). Here the track was down to 80 feet and briefly strayed to the southern bank of the river, to avoid the town centre.

A picturesque stretch through undulating ground requiring cuttings and embankments led to Dairsie (8.5 miles) where Clatto Hill with Kemback Hill dominated old watermills alongside the Eden. More earthworks took the track down to bridges over Moonzie Burn and Motray Water, followed by Leuchars station (12.5 miles) less than 50 feet above sea level. The remainder of the route lay across Tent's Muir, a wild flat peninsula where occasional spinneys and isolated farms on improved pasture punctuated miles of barren land, exposed to the full force of North Sea gales. Much of the rough ground was eventually taken up by the huge Tentsmuir Forest. The railway finally curved north westwards and terminated at the harbour, affording views of Larick Scalp Sands, Pile Lighthouse and Broughty Ferry across the estuary.

Some £85,000 was spent on harbour improvements and new boats, enabling the full ferry service to commence in May 1851. On 14th January 1849 (eleven weeks before it became the Edinburgh, Perth & Dundee Railway) the Edinburgh & Northern had taken on Thomas Bouch as manager and engineer. His first task was to tackle the cumbersome tran-

Despite its early closure in 1921, Leuchars Old station had managed to avoid demolition for over 34 years as B1 4-6-0 No 61403 sauntered through with the 2.17pm Dundee Tay Bridge to Edinburgh Waverley via Tayport on 31st December 1955.

A Metro-Cammell twin forming the 4.59pm for Dundee Tay Bridge leaving Tayport on 27th March 1965. The harbour where the railway boats left for Broughty Ferry is in the background.

shipment process; this was hampering the operation of the Granton-Burntisland ferry and also promised to impede the Tayport-Broughty ferry crossing. His solution was ingenious and transformed the company's prospects. It seems that design work on a train ferry began before Bouch was formally appointed by the Edinburgh & Northern, the *Perth Courier* reporting in December 1848 that a 'floating railroad' was under construction at Govan. The LEVIATHAN was a 399 ton paddle steamer, 180 feet long and 35 feet wide, with funnels at the side giving a clear deck equipped with three lines of rails. She was double ended and had independently operated paddles allowing maximum manoeuvrability.

Although LEVIATHAN was built for use on the Tay, it was decided to employ her on the Forth crossing at the last minute. The new vessel proved a tremendous success and a slightly smaller train ferry was ordered for the Tayport service immediately. Traffic between Edinburgh and Dundee reached enormous proportions, the North British thus inheriting a maritime problem of a different kind from the Edinburgh, Perth & Dundee. Fog and storms occasionally caused delay, but the sheer number of wagons which had to be loaded and unloaded by the shore-based stationary steam engines frequently exceeded the capacity of the system. Consignments were sometimes delayed for weeks and whole trains had to be handed over to the Caledonian for the journey north. A bridge was the only solution - but more of that later.

D49 4-4-0 No 62708 ARGYLLSHIRE leaves Leuchars Junction in charge of the 12.44pm from St Andrews to Glasgow Queen Street Low Level on 9th August 1958. The train reversed here and was brought in by C16 4-4-2T No 67501. A B1 waits in the bay and, as was usually the case, rakes of non-corridor stock occupied the sidings.

St Andrews is one of the most attractive and fascinating towns in Scotland. It enjoys a beautiful setting overlooking a broad bay in the north east corner of Fife, but its turbulent history is symbolised by the ruins of the once magnificent cathedral. The university (founded in 1412) is the oldest north of the border, whilst the Royal and Ancient Club had its origins back in 1754 when golf came to Tayside. By the late 1840s St Andrews had nearly 7,500 inhabitants and was clearly a potential source of traffic for the growing railway network. The Edinburgh & Northern actually gained parliamentary approval for a branch to the town in 1847, but these powers were allowed to lapse.

As was often the case, it was left to local worthies to promote and build their own line. The St Andrews Railway secured its Act on 3rd July 1851 and construction of the 4.5 mile branch from Leuchars to a corner of the Royal and Ancient course was supervised from an office in the town. Thomas Bouch assumed responsibility and work proceeded rapidly.

Overlooked by the trees of the Seggie estate, B1 4-6-0 No 61342 leans into the curve as it crosses the River Eden at Guard Bridge, with the 11.08am Glasgow Buchanan Street to St Andrews on 9th August 1958. The train reversed at Leuchars Junction.

The line opened on 1st July 1852 and was worked by the Edinburgh, Perth & Dundee which provided a new Leuchars station nearer the junction. Unfortunately this suffered from both meagre amenities and poor connections, resulting in a succession of complaints from the local company. The St Andrews Railway itself came under fire when it published a leaflet on the delights of the town, thus encouraging excursionists - some of whom were drunk!

Most of the single track branch was less than 20 feet above high water mark and hugged the shoreline. From Leuchars Junction it turned south and immediately crossed the Moonzie Burn. Guard Bridge station (a mile from Leuchars Junction) preceded a curved viaduct over the tidal River Eden, the largest engineering work on the line. With the Eden estuary to the north and the lower slopes of Clatto Hill to the south, the railway headed east towards the distinctive skyline of St Andrews. The line prospered as predicted, but it could only take very light 0-4-0 locomotives. Following amalgamation with the North British in 1877, the flimsy track was replaced and both timber bridges were rebuilt in iron. A new through station was provided when the Fife Coast line via Crail was completed in 1887. St Andrews always enjoyed a good service of 18 or so trains each way, a few of which were through workings between Dundee and Edinburgh.

THE TAY BRIDGE

Thomas Bouch left the Edinburgh, Perth & Dundee after five years to start his own consultancy in Edinburgh. He championed the idea of bridges across the Tay and Forth from the outset, an ambition clearly well beyond the resources of the company. However, the Edinburgh-Dundee journey by the direct route was becoming an arduous experience for regular passengers (even the best service took well over three hours) and many people opted to travel via Perth. Meanwhile, goods traffic continued to suffer chronic delays. Following the North British takeover in 1862 the Tay Bridge scheme received closer scrutiny, for it seemed the only way of competing with the Caledonian. Bills were presented to parliament in 1864 and 1866, but both failed. Opposition from Dundee Harbour Trustees was the stated reason, although lack of North British confidence in the project must have been apparent. Bouch persisted however, and eventually the idea of a fixed link across the Tay captured the imagination of the directors, as well as Dundee's citizens.

Parliamentary approval came in July 1870 with the proviso that the structure was built upstream of Dundee, thus satisfying the Harbour Trustees. Ships bound for Perth would pass through elevated central spans - the infamous high girders. Few civil engineering firms were willing to tackle such an unprecedented task, but the contract was eventually let to Charles de Bergue & Co. in May 1871. Work began at Wormit on the southern shore and a great abutment of Carmyllie stone gradually grew out of a crag bordering the estuary. One by one, caissons were sunk into the bed of the Tay and men worked in appalling conditions to excavate material for the pier foundations. Once these had been formed, pairs of brick columns were built up to the required height - at least that was the plan.

Bouch had expected to find a solid rock base throughout the crossing, but after just twelve piers had been completed, the bed was made only of thick mud. In fact one bore went down nearly 160 feet and found nothing else. So piles were driven into the sediment and artificial rock bases created. Lighter piers were thus required, and these consisted of lattice girders, adding to the insubstantial appearance of the structure. Most of the spans were cast and fabricated at Wormit, floated out on pontoons and then lifted into place. There were numerous accidents including several fatalities, and on one occasion two spans crashed into the water. Some modifications to the original design were also required as work progressed. The great viaduct gradually took shape, though sceptics found much to criticise. One commented that it looked like 'a cotton thread strung from matchstick to matchstick' against the huge estuary. Another said that it appeared absurdly fragile, 'rising and falling like a switchback'. Since 1874 construction work had been undertaken by Hopkins, Gilkes & Co. after the original contractor pulled out.

The first crossing was made on 26th September 1877 and a subsequent load test using six goods locomotives coupled together was deemed very satisfactory. The finished bridge, 10,395 feet long and just 15 feet wide, had cost £350,000 - double some early estimates. It consisted of 85 spans, the single track running on top of them, with the exception of two bowstring girders at the north end and the thirteen high girders where the rails passed through lattice box structures. A 5.25 mile connecting line was built from Leuchars Junction to the south end of the bridge. This had an easy passage, made possible by a glacial gap at the eastern extremity of the Ochils, and it was here that the isolated station of St Fort was built 3.75 miles from Leuchars Junction. On the north bank, new works included Dundee Tay Bridge station (see Chapter 1).

Regular services between Leuchars Junction and Dundee via the bridge began on 1st June 1878 and North British fortunes took a tremendous leap forward. The company captured a large share of the Edinburgh-Aberdeen passenger business and virtually all coal traffic from Fife to the north passed this way. Journey times from Dundee to the south were cut dramatically and in fact, the railway ferries from Tayport were the only losers. Queen Victoria passed over the Tay Bridge on her way back from Balmoral and Thomas Bouch was knighted shortly afterwards.

On Sunday 28th December 1879 this boundless satisfaction was cruelly snuffed out in a matter of seconds. The collapse of the Tay Bridge shocked the world, and even today the disaster retains a certain notoriety, despite the fact that subsequent disasters have involved greater loss of life.

There was an uneasy calm in the weather over Tayside that Sunday morning, but by late afternoon a wind of unprecedented ferocity was battering Dundee. In his highly evocative book, *The High Girders* (Pan, 1959), John Prebble vividly described the gale: *'Above its eldritch howling there was the continual clatter of falling tiles, the sudden crack and debris-roll of collapsing chimneys. Planks and slates slapped themselves madly against kerbs and walls. Along the shore below the Esplanade the wind ripped off the roofs of bathing huts one by one and either smashed them against the wall or whirled them out into the darkness of the river. An attic roof in Kinloch Street was stripped of its tiles, laths and plaster, and the rain and wind beat in on a screaming tweeny maid.'*

The 5.20pm mail from Burntisland to Dundee, consisting of Wheatley 4-4-0 No 224 hauling five coaches and a brake van, headed north across Fife, its driver and fireman oblivious to the ferocious conditions in the Firth of Tay. By the time the train reached Wormit, all 75 people on board must have been only too aware of the storm, but none of them lived to confirm this. They were claimed by the Tay as it heaved in anger below scudding clouds, punctuated by brief interludes of moonlight.

In Dundee several people were looking out for the train through rain-lashed windows. Some saw flashes of light, presumably from the fire of No 224 as it toppled into the raging water with its train and the thirteen high girders at 7.20pm. Three hours later a steamer set out in the receding gale and North British officials saw the true horror of their shattered bridge at close quarters. Even then there was virtually no hope of finding survivors and, indeed, 29 bodies were never recovered.

The ferries resumed operations the following day and freight traffic had to be handed over to the Caledonian once again. A far reaching enquiry lasting eighteen months concluded that poor foundry work and indifferent maintenance had resulted in the collapse of the box girders when carriages were blown against two of them. It seems that the design had underestimated lateral wind pressure, and excessive train speeds had weakened the structure. Bouch died in October 1880, broken professionally and physically - just like his bridge.

In its short life, the Tay Bridge had proved a public necessity as well as a boon to the North British, so a decision was

A Metro-Cammell triple set forming the 11.48am from Leuchars Junction to St Andrews approaching its destination on 23rd May 1963 in brilliant sunshine. The original St Andrews Railway terminus at a corner of the 'Royal and Ancient' had long been a goods depot, but the original station house on the right and the disused loco shed in the middle distance survived at the time.

A pair of Metro-Cammell triple sets forming the 4.20pm from Dundee Tay Bridge to Edinburgh Waverley passing Wormit signal box on 23rd May 1963. On this fine afternoon, the Tay Bridge, Dundee Law and the Sidlaw Hills formed an attractive backdrop.

soon made to rebuild it. Parliamentary approval came in 1881. Consideration was given to creating a new viaduct on the old foundations, but superstition prevailed and a new structure was planned immediately to the west. It was designed by W H Barlow and the contract was awarded to William Arrol & Co. of Glasgow in April 1882. Although piers and lattice girders were employed again, the second bridge was far stronger than the first and carried double track. Unlike the original fairy-like affair, it looked the part. Civil engineering had progressed considerably in a decade and the contractor was totally reliable, but the cost had escalated to £700,000.

The new structure was 10,711 feet long and consisted of 85 spans, ranging from the eleven 'Wormit arches' at just over 50 feet each to the thirteen 227 feet 'high girders'. From 83 feet above high water mark at the southern end, the bridge descended at 1 in 172, giving a clearance of 79 feet above the main shipping lanes. Ordinary ballasted sleeper track was used, but massive kerbs were provided at the sides to contain any derailed vehicles. The line from Leuchars Junction to Dundee reopened on 20th June 1887, resulting in the final demise of the ferries. There have been no repeats of the incident in December 1879, even during the reckless races to Aberdeen, and the Tay Bridge remains a useful asset to the east coast of Scotland.

NORTH FIFE

One outcome of the Tay Bridge was a remarkably successful commuter line serving residential areas on the south shore. Newport had long been a favourite dormitory village for Dundee businessmen and a ferry plying across the estuary at this point was well used. The Newport Railway was an independent promotion, the aim being to link Tayport with the south end of the bridge at Wormit. It left the former Edinburgh & Northern tracks just short of the harbour and a new through station was provided nearer the centre of Tayport. After curving past cottages overlooking the coast, the single line climbed steadily up the lower slopes of Craig Law. By Newport-on-Tay East station (2.75 miles from Tayport) the rails were 200 feet above sea level. A sharp curve and viaduct across the wooded cleft at Tayfield took the track to Newport-on-Tay West (3.5 miles). A descent past Pluck the Crow Point led to Wormit (5 miles) and another severe curve on to the bridge, 85 feet above the estuary.

The line opened as far as Newport on 12th May 1879, the remaining section to Wormit coming into use the following day. For nearly eight months, local residents had a choice of transport to Dundee, loyalties apparently being shared between the ferries and trains. Unofficial races became the norm, and engine drivers were warned about excessive speed on the Wormit curve and bridge. When the second Tay Bridge opened, the Newport line really came into its own and fully justified the expectations of its promoters. In a couple of decades the population of Newport rose from 1,500 to nearly 4,000 as a direct result of the railway. Edwardian years saw about seventeen trains each way, the first before 6am and the last after 11pm. A high proportion of season tickets from Newport were first class and virtually the only third class fares were from Tayport. It was one of the few Scottish branch lines to have trains on Sundays, and one return working on the Sabbath was strengthened and scheduled to cater for those attending Kirk in Dundee.

Inspired by the success of the Newport Railway, another local concern attempted to develop residential traffic in rural Fife south west of the Tay Bridge, but it failed miserably. The Newburgh & North Fife Railway was authorised on 6th July 1897 and ran into difficulties immediately. A lack of finance meant that construction work did not begin until June 1906, so the company had to ask parliament for an extension of its allotted completion time. The line started at Glenburnie Junction, a mile or so east of Newburgh on the Ladybank-Perth route, and threaded its way through the hills to St Fort between Leuchars Junction and Wormit. It involved a substantial amount of engineering work, including cuttings up to 38 feet deep through glacial deposits. There were no less than 19 underbridges, two of which were lattice girders 66 feet and 81 feet long respectively. An impressive skew span of complex concrete construction carried a road over the formation near Kilmany.

From Glenburnie Junction the line climbed for just over a mile to Lindores station, half of the ascent being as steep as 1 in 70. This was the summit, 250 feet above sea level. A steady descent dominated by Glenduckie Hill and Norman's Law to the north and Dunbog Hill and Mount Hill to the south led to a slight rise into Luthrie station (6 miles). A short drop at 1 in 95, followed by a level section, took the branch to Rathillet Siding at 160 feet. The downhill course continued to Kilmany (10 miles) and St Fort West Junction (altitude 100 feet) where spurs diverged to St Fort North Junction (13˘ miles) and St Andrews Junction on the main line.

The company had purchased sufficient land for double track and laid permanent way capable of taking main line trains. Passenger services commenced on 25th January 1909, goods traffic having begun three days earlier, and an air of optimism prevailed. It was predicted that traffic from St Andrews to Perth and the Highlands would pass over the branch, whilst select residential development in villages such as Kilmany was expected to sustain commuter services into Dundee. The North British worked the Newburgh & North Fife from the outset and there were three trains each way daily, two of them to and from Tay Bridge station. However, a Perth-Dundee 'express' took 47 minutes and could not compete with half hour timings on the Caledonian. Traffic from the productive agricultural land of north Fife provided plenty of work for the sidings and goods yards, but a through night goods was soon discontinued.

The St Andrews-Perth service ceased after just three years and the south to west curve at St Fort was subsequently abandoned. In 1923 the Newburgh & North Fife became part of the LNER. Meanwhile, the original Leuchars station (closed in June 1878 but reopened as Leuchars Old the following December) succumbed on 3rd October 1921. Withdrawal of Newburgh-St Fort passenger services was scheduled for February 1950, but protests to parliament resulted in three postponements. Closure finally took

Top. **It was murky and wet on 30th November 1957 as B1 4-6-0 No 61245 pounded up grade towards the Tay Bridge and disturbed the slumber of Esplanade station. The train was the 1.00pm from Dundee Tay Bridge to Tayport. Although closed to ordinary passenger traffic in 1939, Esplanade was reopened for a few days in June 1957 (along with Magdalen Green on the Perth line) for the Highland Agricultural Show which was held on the nearby links.**

Middle. **Tayport station, looking north west on 27th March 1965, as a Metro-Cammell set forming the 4.27pm from Dundee arrives. The harbour is off to the right.**

Bottom. **A mile or so west of Tayport, Standard 2-6-4T No 80124 climbs the seaward slope of Craig Law with the 6.36pm to Dundee Tay Bridge, on 23rd May 1963. The Tay estuary stretches away to the left.**

place on 12th February 1951, suburban traffic never having materialised. The Glenburnie Junction-Lindores section was abandoned completely on 4th April 1960 and goods services over the rest of the North Fife ceased on 5th October 1964. Dairsie yard closed on the same date, the station having lost its passenger facilities on 20th September 1954. Goods workings to St Fort finished on 2nd November 1964, passenger services following on 6th September 1965 when Guard Bridge station and the Fife Coast line south of St Andrews also closed.

Preparatory work for the Tay Road Bridge meant that buses replaced trains between Tayport and Newport-on-Tay East from 22nd May 1966 until the service was officially withdrawn on 18th December 1967. Tayport Harbour closed to goods on 2nd May 1966, Guard Bridge and St Andrews following shortly on 20th June. There was no respite in 1967, the yards at Newport, Springfield, Wormit and Leuchars Old going on 2nd January, 17th July, 14th August and 6th November respectively. Finally, passenger services between St Andrews and Leuchars Junction ceased on 6th January 1969 and Newport-on-Tay East to Dundee trains ended on 5th May 1969. Springfield, Cupar and Leuchars Junction stations, together with the Ladybank-Dundee line survived the onslaught and remain open today. There is, however, a poignant reminder still of the first line to close - the pier bases of the original Tay Bridge.

Top. **Standard 2-6-4T No 80123 at Newport-on-Tay East with the 5.47pm from Tayport to Dundee Tay Bridge, 23rd May 1963. Brilliant sunshine illuminated comfortable villas overlooking the station, and the attractive Tayport Railway building on the left glowed in reflected light.**

Middle. **A bird's eye view of the neat station at Wormit and the southern end of the Tay Bridge on 17th November 1962. A Derby triple forming the 1.35pm from Arbroath to Tayport makes its first stop on the branch. The main building now forms part of the Scottish Railway Preservation Society station at Bo'ness, being rather improbably attached to the original Edinburgh & Glasgow train shed from Haymarket.**

Bottom. **And finally... Tayside no longer uses trains for short journeys, although most of the basic railway network established a century and a half ago is complete. Dundee once had a number of suburban and local services, but these gradually expired - as outlined earlier. The city also had a fairly extensive tramway system which saw its last workings on 20th October 1956. This was the scene in Nethergate on the last day as car No 44 headed for Ninewells and car No 36 made its way to Maryfield. As in most large urban areas, there have been calls for a return to light rail transport.**